William Hurrell Mallock

Labour and the Popular Welfare

William Hurrell Mallock

Labour and the Popular Welfare

ISBN/EAN: 9783744696548

Printed in Europe, USA, Canada, Australia, Japan

Cover: Foto ©ninafisch / pixelio.de

More available books at **www.hansebooks.com**

LABOUR

AND THE

POPULAR WELFARE

BY

W. H. MALLOCK

AUTHOR OF 'IS LIFE WORTH LIVING,' 'SOCIAL PROBLEMS,' ETC.

LONDON
ADAM AND CHARLES BLACK
1893

PREFACE

NEARLY all the general truths of Economic Science are, directly or indirectly, truths about the character or the actions of human beings. It is, consequently, always well to warn the readers of economic works, that in Political Economy, more than in any other science, every general rule is fringed with exceptions and modifications; and that instances are never far to seek which seem to prove the reverse of what the general rule states, or to make the statement of it appear inaccurate. But such general rules need be none the less true for this; nor for practical purposes any the less safe to reason from. They resemble, in fact, these general truths with regard to the seasons, which we do and must reason from, even in so uncertain a climate as our own. It is, for instance, a truth from which we all reason, that summer is dryer and warmer than winter; and yet there is a frequent occurrence of individual days, which, taken by themselves, contradict it. So, too, those economic definitions, the subjects of which are human actions or faculties, can be entirely accurate only in the *majority* of cases to which they apply; and these cases will be fringed always by a margin of doubtful ones. But the definitions, for all that, need be none the less practically true. Day and night are fringed with doubtful hours of twilight; but our clear knowledge of how midnight differs from noon is not made less clear by our doubts as to whether a certain hour at sunrise ought to be called an hour of night or morning.

It is especially desirable to prefix this

warning to a work as short as the present. In larger and more elaborate works, the writer can particularise the more important exceptions and modifications to which his rules and definitions are subject. But in a short work this task must be left to the common sense of the reader. For popular purposes, however, brevity of statement has one great advantage, namely, that of clearness; and, as the significance of the exceptions cannot be understood without the rules, it is almost essential first to state the rules without obscuring them by the exceptions. There are few readers probably who will not see that the general propositions and principles laid down in the following pages, require, in order to fit them to certain cases, various additions and qualifications. It is necessary only for the reader to bear in mind that these propositions need be none the less broadly and vitally true, because any succinct statement of them is unavoidably incomplete.

CONTENTS

BOOK I

THE DIVISIBLE WEALTH OF THE UNITED KINGDOM

CHAP.   PAGE

I. The Welfare of the Home, as the Logical End of Government 3

II. The Conditions involved in the idea of a Legislative Redistribution of Wealth ; and the Necessary Limitations of the Results . . 14

III. The Pecuniary Results to the Individual of an Equal Division, first of the National Income, and secondly of certain parts of it . . 27

IV. The Nature of the National Wealth : first, of the National Capital ; second, of the National Income. Neither of these is susceptible of Arbitrary Division 49

BOOK II

THE CHIEF FACTOR IN THE PRODUCTION OF THE NATIONAL INCOME

I. Of the various Factors in Production, and how to distinguish the Amount produced by each . 83

CHAP.

II. How the Product of Land is to be distinguished from the Product of Human Exertion . . 92

III. Of the Products of Machinery or Fixed Capital, as distinguished from the Products of Human Exertion 108

IV. Of the Products of Circulating Capital, or Wage Capital, as distinguished from the Products of Human Exertion 122

V. That the Chief Productive Agent in the modern world is not Labour, but Ability, or the Faculty which directs Labour . . 138

VI. Of the Addition made during the last Hundred Years by Ability to the Product of the National Labour. This Increment the Product of Ability 156

BOOK III

AN EXPOSURE OF THE CONFUSIONS IMPLIED IN SOCIALISTIC THOUGHT AS TO THE MAIN AGENT IN MODERN PRODUCTION.

I. The Confusion of Thought involved in the Socialistic Conception of Labour 171

II. That the Ability which at any given period is a Producing Agent, is a Faculty residing in and belonging to living Men . . . 188

III. That Ability is a natural Monopoly, due to the congenital Peculiarities of a Minority. The Fallacies of other Views exposed . . 202

CONTENTS

CHAP. PAGE

IV. The Conclusion arrived at in the preceding Book restated. The Annual Amount produced by Ability in the United Kingdom . . . 228

BOOK IV

THE REASONABLE HOPES OF LABOUR—THEIR MAGNITUDE, AND THEIR BASIS

I. How the Future and Hopes of the Labouring Classes are bound up with the Prosperity of the Classes who exercise Ability . . . 237

II. Of the Ownership of Capital, as distinct from its Employment by Ability . . . 253

III. Of the Causes owing to which, and the Means by which Labour participates in the Growing Products of Ability 273

IV. Of Socialism and Trade Unionism—the Extent and Limitation of their Power in increasing the Income of Labour 291

V. Of the enormous Encouragement to be derived by Labour from a true View of the Situation; and of the Connection between the Interests of the Labourer and Imperial Politics . . 315

BOOK I

THE DIVISIBLE WEALTH OF THE
UNITED KINGDOM

CHAPTER I

The Welfare of the Home, as the Logical End of Government.

I WISH this book to be something which, when the subject of it is considered, the reader perhaps will think it cannot possibly be. For its subject—to describe it in the vague language of the day—is the labour question, the social question, the social claims of the masses; and it is these claims and questions as connected with practical politics. Their connection with politics is close at the present moment; in the immediate future it is certain to become much closer; and yet my endeavour will be to treat them in such a way that men of the most opposite parties—the most progressive Radical and the most old-fashioned Tory—may find this book equally in harmony

The subject of this book, but has nothing to do with party politics.

with their sympathies, and equally useful and acceptable from their respective points of view.

<small>An example of the order of facts it deals with.</small>

But if the reader will consider the matter further, he will see that my endeavour is not necessarily so impracticable as it seems to be. A very little reflection must be enough to show anybody that many of the political problems about which men differ most widely are concerned with an order of truths which, when once they have been examined properly, are the same for all of us; and that a preliminary agreement with regard to them is the only possible basis for any rational disagreement. I will give one example—the land-question. About no political problem is there more disagreement than about this; and yet there are many points in it, about which men may indeed be ignorant, but about which, except for ignorance, there cannot be any controversy. Such for instance is the acreage of the United Kingdom, the number of men by whom the acres are owned, the respective numbers of large and of small properties, together with their respective rentals, and the proportion which the national rent bears to the national income. The truth about all these points is very easily ascertained; and yet not one man in a hundred of those by whom the land-question is discussed, appears to possess the smallest accurate knowledge of it. A curious instance of this ignorance is to be found in the popular reception accorded some years ago to the theories of Mr. Henry George. If Mr. George's reasonings were correct as applied to this country, the rental of our titled and untitled aristocracy would be now about *eight hundred millions:* and few of his admirers quarrelled with this inference. But if they had only consulted official records, and made themselves masters of the real facts of the case, they would have seen at once that this false and ludicrous estimate was wrong by no less a sum than *seven hundred and seventy millions;* that the *eight hundred millions* of Mr. George's fancy were in reality not more than *thirty;* and that the rent, which according to him was two-thirds of the national income, was not in reality more than two and a quarter per cent of it. Now here is a fact most damaging to the authority of a certain theorist with whom many Radicals

[margin: BOOK I. CH. I. Such facts as these not generally known; but when once ascertained, necessarily the same for all parties:]

are no doubt in sympathy; but it none the less is a fact which any honest Radical is as much concerned to know as is any honest Tory, and which may easily supply the one with as many arguments as the other. The Tory may use it against the Radical rhetorician who denounces the landlords as appropriating the whole wealth of the country. The Radical may use it against the Tory who is defending the House of Peers, and may ask why a class whose collective wealth is so small, should be specially privileged to represent the interests of property: whilst those who oppose protection may use it with equal force as showing how the diffusion of property has been affected by free trade.

And it is equally to the advantage of all parties to understand such facts.

Here is a fair sample, so far as particular facts are concerned, of the order of truths with which I propose to deal: and if I can deal with them in the way they ought to be dealt with, they will be as interesting—and many will be as amusing—as they are practically useful. It may indeed be said, without the smallest exaggeration, that the salient facts which underlie our social problems of to-day, would, if properly presented, be to the general reader as stimulating and fresh as any novel or book of travels, besides being as little open to any mere party criticism.

But there are other truths, besides particular facts, which I propose to urge on the reader's attention also. There are general truths, general considerations, and principles: and these too, like the facts, will be found to have this same characteristic—that though many of them are not generally realised, though many of them are often forgotten, and though some of them are supposed to be the possession of this or that party only, they do but require to be fairly and clearly stated, to command the assent of every reflecting mind, and to show themselves as common points from which, like diverging lines, all rational politicians, whatever may be their differences, must start.

The very first principle to which I must call attention, and which forms a key to my object throughout this entire book, will at once be recognised by the reader as being of this kind. The Radical perhaps may regard it as a mere truism; but the most bigoted Tory, on reflection, will not deny that it is

BOOK I. CH. I.

Besides such facts, this book deals with general truths and principles, equally independent of party.

The proposition with which the argument starts is an example of a truth of this kind.

BOOK I.
CH. I.

The conditions of private happiness are the end of all Government.

true. The great truth or principle of which I speak is as follows.

The ultimate end of Government is to secure or provide for the greatest possible number, not indeed happiness, as is often inaccurately said, but the external conditions that make happiness possible. As for happiness, that must come from ourselves, or at all events from sources beyond the control of Governments. But though no external conditions are sufficient to make it come, there are many which are sufficient to drive it or to keep it permanently away; and it is the end of all Government to minimise conditions such as these. Now these conditions, though their details vary in various cases, are essentially alike in all. They are a want of the necessaries, or a want of the decencies of life, or an excessive difficulty in obtaining them, or a recurring impossibility of doing so. They are conditions in fact which principally, though not entirely, result from an uncertain or an insufficient income. The ultimate duty of a Government is therefore towards the incomes of the governed; and the three chief tests of whether a Government is good or bad, are first the number of families

These conditions are principally a question of private income.

The end of Government is

in receipt of sufficient incomes, secondly the security with which the receipt of such incomes can be counted on, and lastly the quality of the things which such incomes will command.

therefore to secure adequate incomes for the greatest possible number.

Some people however—perhaps even some Radicals—may be tempted to say that this is putting the case too strongly, and is caricaturing the truth rather than fairly stating it. They may say that it excludes or degrades to subordinate positions all the loftier ends both of individual and of national life, such as moral and mental culture, and the power and greatness of the country: but in reality it does nothing of the kind.

This view not necessarily materialistic, nor unpatriotic:

In the first place, with regard to moral and mental culture, if these are really desired by the individual citizen, they will be included amongst the things which his income will help him to obtain: and an insufficient income certainly tends to deprive him of them. If he wishes to have books, he must have money to buy books: and if he wishes his children to be educated, there must be money to pay for teaching them. In the second place, with regard to the power and greatness of the

For income is necessary for mental as well as physical welfare,

BOOK I. CH. I.

And the complete welfare of the citizens is what gives meaning to patriotism.

country, though for many reasons we are apt to forget the fact, it is the material welfare of the home, or the maintenance of the domestic income, that really gives to them the whole of their fundamental meaning. Our Empire and our power of defending it have a positive money value, which affects the prosperity of every class in the country: and though this may not be the only ground on which our Empire can be justified, it is the only ground on which, considering what it costs, its maintenance can be justified in the eyes of a critical democracy. Supposing it could be shown to demonstration that the loss of our Empire and our influence would do no injury to our trade, or make one British household poorer, it is impossible to suppose that the democracy of Great Britain would continue for long, from mere motives of sentiment, to sanction the expense, or submit to the anxiety and the danger, which the maintenance of an Empire like our own constantly and necessarily involves.

Further, patriotism will only flourish in a country which

But let us waive this argument, and admit that a sense of our country's greatness, quite apart from any thought of our own material advantage, enlarges and elevates the mind as nothing else can—that to be proud of our country and proud of ourselves as belonging to it, to feel ourselves partners in the majesty of the great battle-ship, in the menace of Gibraltar stored with its sleeping thunders, or the boastful challenge of the flag that floats in a thousand climates, is a privilege which it is easier to underrate than exaggerate. Let us admit all this. But these large and ennobling sentiments are all of them dependent on the welfare of the home in this way:—they are hardly possible for those whose home conditions are miserable. Give a man comfort in even the humblest cottage, and the glow of patriotism may, and probably will, give an added warmth to that which shines on him from his fireside. But if his children are crying for food, and he is shivering by a cold chimney, he will not find much to excite him in the knowledge that we govern India. Thus, from whatever point of view we regard the matter, the welfare of the home as secured by a sufficient income is seen to be at once the test and the end of Government; and it ceases to be the end of patriotism only when it becomes the foundation of it.

BOOK I.
CH. I.

secures for its citizens the conditions of a happy life.

BOOK I.
CH. I.

Cupidity, therefore, or the desire for sufficient income, is a legitimate basis for popular interest in politics;

Here, then, is the principle which I assume throughout this volume. And now, I think that, having explained it thus, I may, without offence to either Tory or Radical, venture to condemn, as strongly as its stupidity deserves, the way in which politicians are at present so often attacked for appealing to what is called the cupidity of the poorer classes. Cupidity is in itself the most general and legitimate desire to which any politician or political party can appeal. It is illegitimate only when it is excited by illegitimate methods: and these methods are of two obvious kinds. One is an exaggeration of the advantages which are put before the people as obtainable: the other is the advocacy of a class of measures as means to them, by which not even a part of them could be, in reality, obtained. Everybody must see that a cupidity which is excited thus is one of the most dangerous elements by which the prosperity of a country can be threatened. But a cupidity which is excited in the right way, which is controlled by a knowledge of what wealth really exists, and of the fundamental conditions on which its distribution depends—is merely another name for spirit, energy, and intelligence.

My one aim then, in writing this book, is to educate the cupidity of voters, no matter what their party, by popularising knowledge of this non-controversial kind. And such knowledge will be found, as I have said already, to be composed partly of particular facts, and partly of general truths. We will begin with the consideration of certain particular facts, which must, however, be prefaced by a few general observations.

BOOK I. CH. I.

The aim of this book is to educate popular cupidity.

CHAPTER II

The Conditions involved in the idea of a Legislative Redistribution of Wealth; and the Necessary Limitations of the Results.

<small>All men ask of a Government either the increase or the maintenance of their incomes.</small>

LET me then repeat that we start with assuming cupidity as not only the general foundation, but also as the inevitable, the natural, and the right foundation, of the interest which ordinary men of all classes take in politics. We assume that where the ordinary man, of whatever class or party, votes for a member of Parliament, or supports any political measure, he is primarily actuated by one of two hopes, or both of them—the first being the hope of securing the continuance of his present income, the second being the hope of increasing it. Now, to secure what they have already got is the hope of all classes; but to increase it by legislation is the hope of the poorer only. It is of course perfectly true that the rich as well as the poor are anxious, as a rule, to increase their incomes when they can; but they expect to do so by their own ability and enterprise, and they look to legislation for merely such negative help as may be given by affording their abilities fair play.

But with the poorer classes the case is entirely different. They look to legislation for help of a direct and positive kind, which may tend to increase their incomes, without any new effort of their own: and not only do they do this themselves, but the richer classes sympathise with the desire that makes them do so. It is, for instance, by no means amongst the poorer classes only that the idea of seizing on the land, without compensating the owners, has found favour as a remedy for distress and poverty generally. Owners of every kind of property, except land, have been found to advocate it; whilst as to such vaguer and less startling proposals, as the "restoration of the labourer to the soil," the limitation of the hours of labour, or the gradual acquirement by the State of many of our larger industries—the persistent way in which these

The poor alone look for an increase of income by direct legislative means. They are right in doing this.

are being kept before the public, is due quite as much to men of means as to poor men. It is then with the cupidity of the poorer classes that we are chiefly concerned to deal; and the great question before us may briefly be put thus: By what sort of social legislation may the incomes of the poorer classes—or, in other words, the incomes of the great mass of the community—be, in the first place, made more constant; and, in the second place, increased?

But before proceeding to this inquiry, there is a preliminary question to be disposed of. What is the maximum increase which any conceivable legislation could conceivably secure for them out of the existing resources of the country? Not only unscrupulous agitators, but many conscientious reformers, speak of the results to be hoped for from a better distribution of riches, in terms so exaggerated as to have no relation to facts; and ideas of the wildest kind are very widely diffused as to the degree of opulence which it would be possible to secure for all. The consequence is that at the present moment popular cupidity has no rational standard. It will therefore be well, before we go further, to reduce these ideas—I do not say to the limits which facts will warrant—but to the limits which facts set on what is theoretically and conceivably possible.

An ascertainable limit is placed to this amount by circumstances.

Let me then call attention to the self-evident truth, that the largest income which could possibly be secured for everybody, could not be more than an equal share of the actual gross income enjoyed by the entire nation. Now it happens that we know with substantial accuracy what the gross amount of the income of the nation now is, and I will presently show what is the utmost which each individual could hope for from the most successful attempt at a redistribution of everything. But the mere pecuniary results of a revolution of this kind are not the only results of which we must take account. There are others which it will be well to glance at before proceeding to our figures.

And this amount would be obtainable only under certain conditions,

Though an equal division of wealth would, as we soon shall see, bring a large addition to the income of a considerable majority of the nation, the advantages which the recipients would gain from this addition, would be very different from the advantages which

One of which would entirely change the existing character of wealth.

an individual would gain now, from the same annual sum coming to him from invested capital. In other words, if wealth were equally distributed, it would, from the very necessity of the case, lose half the qualities for which it is at present most coveted.

At present wealth suggests before all things what is commonly called "an independence"—something on which a man can live independently of his own exertions. But the moment a whole nation possessed it in equal quantities this power of giving an independence would go from it suddenly and for ever. If a workman who at present makes *seventy pounds* a year, would receive, by an equal division, an additional *forty pounds*, it is indeed true that no additional work could be entailed on him. The work which at present gets him *seventy pounds*, would in that case get him *a hundred and ten*. But he would never be able, if he preferred leisure to wealth, to forego the *seventy pounds* and live in idleness on the *forty pounds;* as he would be able to do now if the additional *forty pounds* were the interest of a legacy left him by his maiden aunt. Unless he continued to work, as he had worked hitherto, he would lose not only the first sum, but the second.

This is self-evident, when we consider what is the essence of such a situation, namely that the position of everybody is identical. For if everybody preferred to be idle, no wealth could be produced at all. However great nominally might be the value of our national property, it is perfectly clear that everybody could not live at leisure in it: and from the very nature of the case, in a nation where all are equal, what cannot be done by all, could not be done by anybody. If, therefore, we estimate the income possible for each individual as an equal fraction of the present income of the nation, it must be remembered that, to produce the total out of which these fractions are to come, everybody would have to work as hard as he does now. And more than that, it would be the concern of all to see that his share of work was not being shirked by anybody. This is at present the concern of the employer only: but under the conditions we are now considering, everybody would be directly interested in becoming his neighbour's taskmaster.

BOOK I.
CH. II.

These last considerations lead us to another aspect of the subject, with which every intelligent voter should make himself thoroughly familiar, and which every honest speaker would force on the attention of his hearers. A large number of agitators, who are either ignorant or entirely reckless, but who nevertheless possess considerable gifts of oratory, are constantly endeavouring to associate, in the popular mind, the legitimate hope of obtaining an increased income, with an insane hostility to conditions which alone make such an increase possible. These men[1] are accustomed to declaim against the slavery of the working classes, quite as much as against their inadequate rate of payment. By slavery they mean what they call "enslavement to capital." Capital means the implements and necessaries of production. These, they argue, are no longer owned by the workmen as they were in former times: and thus the workers are no longer their own masters. They must work

And be even more under the dominion of the employer than he is now;

---

[1] Writers also from whom better things might have been expected make use of the same foolish language. "The proletarian, in accepting the highest bid, sells himself openly into bondage" (*Fabian Essays*, p. 12).

under the direction of those who can give them the means of working; and this, they are urged to believe, reduces them to the condition of slaves.

Of course, in these representations there is a certain amount of truth: but it is difficult to conceive of anything more stupidly and more wantonly misleading, than the actual meaning which they are employed by the agitators to convey. For that meaning is nothing else than this—that under improved conditions, when wealth is better distributed, the so-called slavery will disappear, the workers will be their own masters again, and will each own, as formerly, the implements and the materials of his work. But, as no one knows better than the extreme socialists, and as any intelligent man can see easily for himself, such a course of events is not only not possible, but is the exact reverse of that on which the progress of the workers must depend. The wildest agitator admits, and the most ignorant agitator knows, that the wealth of the modern world, on the growth of which they insist, and which, for the very reason that its growth has been so enormous, is declared by them

Nor could any one hope to own the instruments of production used by him.

Self-contradictions of agitators, who say that capitalism means slavery, and that socialism

would make the worker free.

to offer so rich a prize to the workers, mainly owes its existence to improved conditions of production. Such persons know also that of these conditions the chief have been the development of machinery, the increased subdivision of employments, and the perfected co-operation of the workers. But the development of machinery necessarily means this—the transformation of (say) each thousand old-fashioned implements into a single vast modern one of a hundred times their aggregate power : and it means that at this single implement a thousand men shall work. The increased subdivision of labour means that no man shall make an entire thing, but merely some small part of it; and perfected co-operation is another name for perfected discipline. It will be thus seen that the conditions which the agitator calls those of slavery are essential to the production of the wealth which is to constitute the workers' heritage. It will be seen that the workers' hope of bettering their own position is so far from depending on a recovery of any former freedom, that it involves yet further elaboration of industrial discipline ; and puts the old

The industrial discipline of the State would necessarily be much harder than ownership of his own tools by the individual further and further away into the region of dreams and impossibilities: and that no redistribution of wealth would even tend to bring it back again. The weaver of the last century was the owner of his own loom: and a great cotton-mill may now be owned by one capitalist. But a co-operative cotton-mill that was owned by all the workers, in the old sense of the word would not be owned by anybody. Could any one of these thousand or more men say that any part of the mill was his own personal property? Could he treat a single bolt, or a brick, or a wheel, or a doornail, as he might have treated a loom left to him in his cottage by his father? Obviously not. No part of the mill would be his own private property, any more than a train starting from Euston Station is the property of any shareholder in the London and NorthWestern Railway. His ownership would mean merely that he was entitled to a share of the profits, and that he had one vote out of a thousand in electing the managers. But however the managers were elected, he would have to obey their orders; and their discipline

that of the private employer.

would be probably stricter than that of any private owner. Much more would this be the case if the dream of the Socialist were fulfilled, and if instead of each factory or business being owned by its own workers, all the workers of the country collectively owned all the businesses—all the machinery, all the raw materials, and all the capital reserved for and spent in wages. For though the capital of the country would be owned by the workers nominally, their use of it would have to be regulated by a controlling body, namely the State. The managers and the taskmasters would all be State officials, and be armed with the powers of the State to enforce discipline. The individual under such an arrangement, might gain in point of income; but if he is foolish enough to adopt the view of the agitator, and regard himself as the slave to capital now, he would be no less a slave to it were all capitals amalgamated, and out of so many million shares he himself were to own one.

It is particularly desirable in this particular place to fix the reader's attention on this aspect of the question, because it is inseparably associated with the point we are preparing to consider—namely, the pecuniary position in which the individual would be placed by an equal division, were such possible, of the entire national income. For we must bear in mind that not even in thought or theory is an equal division of the national income possible, unless all the products of the labour of every citizen are in the first place taken by the State as sole employer and capitalist, and are then distributed as wages in equal portions. Under no other conditions could equality be more than momentary. If each worker himself sold his own products to the consumer,—which he could not do, because no one produces the whole of anything,—the strong and industrious would soon be richer than the idle; and the man with no children richer than the man with ten. Inequality would have begun again as soon as one day's work was over. Equality demands, as the Socialists are well aware, that all incomes shall be wages paid by the State; and it implies further, as we shall presently have occasion to observe—that equal wages shall be paid to all individuals, not because they are equally productive, but because they are all equally human. When

[Marginal note: BOOK I. CH. II. —tion of wealth necessarily presupposes the State as sole employer and capitalist.]

therefore I speak, as I shall do presently, of what each individual would receive, if wealth were divided equally, I must be understood as meaning that he would receive so much from the State.

A redistribution of wealth, if it increased the incomes of some, would lessen the labour of nobody.

Let us remember then that a redistribution of wealth would have in itself no tendency to alter the existing conditions of the workers in any respect except that of wages only. It would not tend to relieve any man of a single hour of labour, to give him any more freedom in choosing the nature of his work or the method of it, or make him less liable to fines or other punishments for disobedience or unpunctuality. His only gain, if any, would be a simple gain in money. Let us now proceed to deal with the pounds, shillings, and pence; and see what is the utmost that this gain could come to.

The next chapter contains an examination of the amount of income which would theoretically result from an equal distribution in this country.

CHAPTER III

The Pecuniary Results to the Individual of an Equal Division, first of the National Income, and secondly of certain parts of it.

THE gross income of the United Kingdom— the aggregate yearly amount received by the entire population — is computed to be in round numbers some *thirteen hundred million pounds.* But though this estimate may be accepted as true under existing circumstances, we should find it misleading as an estimate of the amount available for distribution. So far as it relates to the income of the poorer classes, it would be indeed still trustworthy; but the income of the richer—which is the total charged with income-tax—we should find to be seriously exaggerated, as considerable sums are included in it which are counted twice over. For instance, the fee

The gross income of the United Kingdom.

28 THE INCOME OF GREAT BRITAIN

BOOK I.
CH. III.

The whole amount attributed to the rich would not be available for distribution.

of a great London doctor for attending a patient in the South of France would be about *twelve hundred pounds*. Let us suppose this to be paid by a patient whose income is *twelve thousand pounds*. The doctor pays income-tax on his fee; the patient pays income-tax on his entire income; and thus the whole sum charged with income-tax is *thirteen thousand two hundred pounds*. But if we came to distribute it, we should find that there was *twelve thousand pounds* only. And there are many other cases of a precisely similar nature. According to the calculations of Professor Leone Levi, the total amount which was counted twice over thus, amounted ten years ago to more than *a hundred million pounds*.[1] In order, therefore, to arrive at the sum which we may assume to be susceptible of distribution, it will be necessary, therefore, to deduct at least as

[1] According to Professor Leone Levi, the actual sum would be *one hundred and thirteen million pounds*: but in dealing with estimates such as these, in which absolute accuracy is impossible, it is better, as well as more convenient, to use round numbers. More than nine-tenths of this sum belongs to the income of the classes that pay income-tax. Of the working-class income, not more than two per cent is counted twice over, according to Professor Leone Levi.

much as this from the sum which was just now mentioned of *thirteen hundred million pounds*.[1] Accordingly the income of the country, if we estimate it with a view to dividing it, is in round numbers, *twelve hundred million pounds*.

A certain deduction must therefore be made from the estimated total.

And now let us glance at our problem in its crudest and most rudimentary form, and see what would be the share coming to each individual, if these millions were divided equally amongst the entire population. The entire population of the United Kingdom numbers a little over *thirty-eight millions*; so our division sum is simple. The share of each individual would be about *thirty-two pounds*. But this sort of equality in distribution would satisfy nobody. It is not worth talking about. For a quarter of the population are children under ten years of age,[2] and nearly two-fifths are under fifteen: and it would be absurd to assign to a baby seeking a pap-bottle, or even to a boy—vora-

This, divided amongst all, would yield thirty-two pounds per head:

---

[1] There is a general agreement amongst statisticians with regard to these figures. *Cf.* Messrs Giffen, Mulhall, and Leone Levi *passim*.

[2] Out of any *thousand* inhabitants, *two hundred and fifty-eight* are under ten years of age; and *three hundred and sixty-six* out of every *thousand* are under fifteen.

30 HOW TO DIVIDE THE INCOME EQUALLY

BOOK I.
CH. III.

But different sexes and ages would require different amounts,

cious as boys' appetites are—the same sum that would be assigned to a full-grown man or woman. In order to give our distribution even the semblance of rationality, the shares must be graduated according to the requirements of age and sex. The sort of proportion to each other which these graduated shares should bear might possibly be open to some unimportant dispute: but we cannot go far wrong if we take for our guide the amount of food which scientific authorities tell us is required respectively by men, women, and children; together with the average proportion which actually obtains at present, both between their respective wages and the respective costs of their maintenance.

The proportions of which are readily ascertainable.

The result which we arrive at from these sources of information is substantially as follows, and every fresh inquiry confirms it. For every *pound* which is required or received by a man, *fifteen shillings* does or should go to a woman, *ten shillings* to a boy, *nine shillings* to a girl, and *four and sixpence* to an infant.[1]

---

[1] Statistics in support of the above result might be indefinitely multiplied, both from European countries and America. So far as food is concerned, scientific authorities

SHARES OF MEN, WOMEN, AND CHILDREN

So much, then, being admitted, we shall make our calculations best by starting with the family as our unit, and coming to the individual afterwards. The average family consists of four and a half persons; and the families in the United Kingdom number *eight and a half millions*. *Twelve hundred millions* —the sum we have to divide—would give each family an income of *a hundred and forty pounds*. From this, however, we should have to deduct taxes; and, since if all classes were equal, all would have to be taxed equally,— the amount due from each family would be considerable. Public expenditure, if the State directed everything, would of necessity be larger than it is at present; but even if we assume that it would remain at its present figure, each family would have to contribute at least *sixteen pounds*.[1] Therefore *sixteen*

The problem best approached by taking the family as the unit:

tell us that if *twenty* represents the amount required by a man, a woman will require *fifteen*, and a child *eleven ;* but the total expenditures necessary are somewhat different in proportion.

[1] The total imperial taxation in the United Kingdom is about *two pounds eight shillings* per head ; and the total local taxation is about *one pound four shillings.* Thus the two together come to *three pounds twelve shillings* per head, which for every family of four and a half persons gives a total of *sixteen pounds four shillings.*

pounds must be deducted from the *hundred and forty pounds*. Accordingly we have for four and a half persons a net income of *a hundred and twenty-six pounds*. Now these persons would be found to consist on an average of a man and his wife, a youth, a girl, and a half of a baby,—for when we deal with averages we must execute many judgments like Solomon's,—and if we distribute the income among them in the proportion I just now indicated, the result we shall arrive at will, in round numbers, be this. The man will have *fifty pounds*, the woman *thirty-six pounds*, the youth *twenty-five pounds*, the girl *twenty-four pounds*, and the half of the infant *five pounds*. And now let us scrutinise the result a little further, and see how it looks in various familiar lights. An equal distribution of the whole wealth of the country would give every adult male about *nineteen shillings and sixpence* a week, and every adult female about *fourteen shillings*. These sums would, however, be free of taxes; so in order to compare them with the wages paid at present, we must add to them *two shillings and sixpence* and *two shillings* respectively, which will raise them respectively to *twenty-two shillings*, and to *sixteen shillings:* but a bachelor who is earning the former sum now, or an unmarried woman who is now earning the latter, would neither of them, under any scheme of equal distribution conceivable, come in for a penny of the plunder taken from the rich. They already are receiving all that, on principles of equality, they could claim.

_{BOOK I.}
_{CH. III.}

The maximum income that an equal distribution would give a bachelor.

The smallness of this result is likely to startle anybody; but none the less is it true: and it is well to consider it carefully, because the reason why it startles us requires to be particularly noticed. Of the female population of the country that is above fifteen years old, the portion that works for wages is not so much as a half;[1] and of the married women that do so, the portion is much smaller. The remainder work, no doubt, quite as hard as the rest; but they work as wives and mothers; and whatever money they have comes to them through their husbands. Thus when the ordinary man considers the question of income, he regards

---

[1] The number of females over fifteen years of age is about *twelve millions*. Those who work for wages number less than *five millions*.

income as something which belongs exclusively to the man, his wife and his children being things which the man maintains as he pleases. But the moment the principle of equality of distribution is accepted, all such ideas as these have to be rudely changed: for if all of us have a claim to an equal share of wealth, just as the common man's claim is as good as that of the uncommon man, so the woman's claim is as good as the claim of either; and whatever her income might be under such conditions, it would be hers in her own right, not in that of anybody else. Accordingly it happens that an equal distribution of wealth, though it would increase the present income of the ordinary working man's family, might actually, so far as the head of the family was concerned, have the paradoxical result of making him feel that personally he was poorer than before—not richer.[1]

[1] Mr. Giffen's latest estimates show that not more than twenty-three per cent of the wage-earners in this country earn less than *twenty shillings* a week; whilst seventy-seven per cent earn this sum and upwards. Thirty-five per cent earn from *twenty shillings* to *twenty-five shillings;* and forty-one per cent earn more than *twenty-five shillings*. See evidence given by Mr. Giffen before the Labour Commission, 7th December 1892.

The man's personal share, then, would be *twenty-two shillings* a week, and the woman's *sixteen shillings;* and they could increase their income in no way except by marrying. As many of their expenses would be greatly diminished by being shared, they would by this arrangement both be substantial gainers: but if the principle of equality were properly carried out, they would gain very little further by the appearance of children; for though we must assume that a certain suitable sum would be paid them by the State for the maintenance of each child, that would have to be spent for the child's benefit. We may, therefore, say that the utmost results which could possibly be secured to the individual by a general confiscation and a general redistribution of wealth, would be represented by the condition of a childless man and wife, with *thirty-eight shillings* a week, which they could spend entirely on themselves: for all the wealth of the nation that was not absorbed in supplying such incomes to men and women who were childless, would be absorbed in supporting the children of those who had them; thus merely equalising

BOOK I.
CH. III.
—
The highest possible standard of living would be represented by a man and wife without children.

the conditions of large and of small families, and enabling the couple with ten or a dozen children to be personally as well off as the couple with none. Could such a condition of wellbeing be made universal, many of the darkest evils of civilisation would no doubt disappear: but it is well for a man who imagines that the masses of this country are kept by unjust laws out of the possession of some enormous heritage, to see how limited would be the result, if the laws were to give them everything; and to reflect that the largest income that would thus be assigned to any woman, would be less than the income enjoyed at the present moment by multitudes of unmarried girls who work in our Midland mills—girls whose wages amount to *seventeen shillings* a week, who pay their parents *a shilling* a day for board, and who spend the remainder, with a most charming taste, on dress.

He will have to reflect also that such a result as has been just described could be produced only by an equality that would be absolutely grotesque in its completeness—by every male being treated as equal to every other male of the same age, and by every female being treated similarly. The prime minister, the commander-in-chief, the most important State official, would thus, if they were unmarried, be poorer than many a factory-girl is at present; whilst if they were married, they and their wives together would have but *four shillings* a week more than is at present earned by a mason, and *six shillings* a week less than is earned by an overlooker in a cotton-mill.

But an equality of this kind, from a practical point of view, is worth considering only as a means of reducing it to an absurdity. Even were it established to-morrow, it could not be maintained for a month, owing to the difficulty that would arise in connection with the question of children: as unless a State official checked the weekly bills of every parent, parents inevitably would save out of their children's allowances; and those with many children would be very soon founding fortunes. And again it is obvious that different kinds of occupation require from those engaged in them unequal expenditures; so that the inevitable inequality of needs would make pecuniary

Absolute pecuniary equality, however, is not thought possible by anybody;

> As the salaries asked for Members of Parliament by the Labour Party how.

equality impossible. Indeed every practical man in our own country owns this, however extreme his views; as is evidenced by the amounts which have been suggested by the leaders of the Labour Party as a fit salary for a paid Member of Parliament. These amounts vary from *three hundred pounds* a year to *four hundred pounds;* so that the unmarried Member of Parliament, in the opinion of our most thoroughgoing democrats, deserves an income from six to eight times as great as the utmost income possible for the ordinary unmarried man. And there are many occupations which will, if this be admitted, deserve to be paid on the same or on even a higher scale. We may therefore take it for granted that the most levelling politicians in the country, with whom it is worth while to reason as practical and influential men, would spare those incomes not exceeding *four hundred pounds* a year, and would probably increase the number of those between that amount and *a hundred and fifty pounds.* Now the total amount of the incomes between these limits is not far from *two hundred million pounds:* so if this be deducted from the *twelve hundred million pounds* which we just now took as the sum to be divided equally, the incomes of the people at large will be less by sixteen per cent than the sums at which they were just now estimated; and the standard of average comfort will be represented by a childless man and wife having *thirty-one shillings and eightpence* instead of *thirty-eight shillings* a week.

We need not, however, dwell upon such details longer: for there are few people who conceive even a redistribution like this to be possible; and there would probably be fewer still who would run the risk of attempting it, if they realised how limited would be the utmost results of it to themselves. My only reason for dealing with these schemes at all is that, whilst they are felt to be impossible as soon as they are considered closely, they are yet the schemes which invariably suggest themselves to the mind when first the idea of any great social change is presented to it; and a knowledge of their theoretical results, though it offers no indication of what may actually be attainable, will sober our thoughts, and at the same time stimulate them, by putting a distinct and business-like limit to what is conceivable.

40   THE ATTACK ON

BOOK I.   And for this reason, before I proceed
CH. III.
further, I shall ask the reader to consider a
But there
are certain few more theoretical estimates. The popular
parts of the
national agitator, and those whose opinions are influ-
income the
redistribu- enced by him, do not propose to seize upon
tion of
which has all property; they content themselves with
been
actually proposing to appropriate certain parts of it.
advocated,
i.e. : The parts generally fixed upon are as follows :
(1) the rent
of the land; —First and foremost comes the landed rental [1]
(2) the in-
terest of the of the country—the incomes of the iniquitous
National
Debt ; landlords. Second comes the interest on the
(3) the
sums spent National Debt; third, the profits of the railway
on the
Monarchy. companies ; and last, the sum that goes to
support the Monarchy. All these annual sums
have been proposed as subjects of confiscation,
though the process may generally be disguised

[1] The reader must observe that I speak of the *rent* of the land, not of the land itself, as the subject of the above calculation. I forbear to touch the question of any mere change in the occupancy or administration of the land, or even of any scheme of nationalising the land by purchasing it at its market price from the owners ; for by none of these would the present owners be robbed pecuniarily, nor would the nation pecuniarily gain, except in so far as new conditions of tenure made agriculture more productive. All such schemes are subjects of legitimate controversy, or, in other words, are party questions; and I therefore abstain from touching them. I deal in the text with facts about which there can be no controversy.

under other names. Let us take each of these separately, and see what the community at large would gain by the appropriation of each. And we will begin with the income of the landlords; for not only is this the property which is most frequently attacked, but it is the one from the division of which the largest results are expected. It is indeed part of the creed of a certain type of politician that, if the income of the landlords could be only divided amongst the people, all poverty would be abolished, and the great problem solved.

BOOK I. CH. III.

We will consider what the nation would gain by confiscating the above.

Absurd ideas as to the amount of the landed rental of the country.

In the minds of most of our extreme reformers, excepting a few Socialists, the income of the landlords figures as something limitless; and the landlords themselves as the representatives of all luxury. It is not difficult to account for this. To any one who studies the aspect of any of our rural landscapes, with a mind at all occupied with the problem of the redistribution of wealth, the things that will strike his eye most and remain uppermost in his mind, are the houses and parks and woods belonging to the large landlords. Small houses and cottages, though he might see a hundred of them in a three-miles' drive, he

The popular conception of the wealth of the larger landlords.

would hardly notice; but if in going from York to London he caught glimpses of twelve large castles, he would think that the whole of the Great Northern Railway was lined with them. And from impressions derived thus two beliefs have arisen—first that the word "landlord" is synonymous with "large landlord"; and secondly that large landlords own most of the wealth of the kingdom. But ideas like these, when we come to test them by facts, are found to be ludicrous in their falsehood. If we take the entire rental derived from land, and compare it with the profits derived from trade and capital, we shall find that, so far as mere money is concerned, the land offers the most insignificant, instead of the most important question[1] that could engage us. Of the income of the nation, the entire rental of the land does not amount to more than one-thirteenth; and during the last

[1] It is also every year becoming more unimportant, in diametrical contradiction of the theories of Mr. H. George. This was pointed out some twelve years ago by Professor Leone Levi, who showed that whereas in 1814 the incomes of the landlord and farmer were fifty-six per cent of the total assessed to income-tax, in 1851 they were thirty-seven per cent, and in 1880 only twenty-four per cent. They are now only sixteen per cent.

THE REAL RENTAL OF THE LANDLORDS 43

ten years it has fallen about thirteen per cent. The community could not possibly get more than all of it; and if all of it were divided in the proportions we have already contemplated, it would give each man about twopence a day and each woman about three half-pence.[1]

But the more important part of the matter still remains to be noticed. The popular idea is, as I just now said, that we should, in confiscating the rental of the kingdom, be merely robbing a handful of rich men, who would be probably a deserving, and certainly an easy prey. The facts of the case are, however, singularly different. It is true, indeed, if we reckon the land by area, that the large landlords own a preponderating part of it: but if we reckon the land by value, the whole case is reversed; and we find that classes of men who are supposed by the ordinary agitator to have no fixed interest in the national soil at all, really draw from it a rental twice as great as that of the class which is supposed to absorb the whole. I will give the actual figures,[2]

The landed aristocracy are not the chief rent-receivers.

A multitude of small proprietors receive twice as much in rent as the entire landed aristocracy.

BOOK I.
CH. III.

---

[1] See Local Government Board valuation of 1878.
[2] Recent falls in rent make it impossible to give the

based upon official returns; and in order that the reader may know my exact meaning, let me define the term that I have just used—namely "large landlords"—as meaning owners of more than *a thousand* acres. No one, according to popular usage, would be called a large landlord, who was not the owner of at least as much as this; indeed the large landlord, as denounced by the ordinary agitator, is generally supposed to be the owner of much more. Out of the aggregate rental, then—that total sum which would, if divided, give each man twopence a day—what goes to the large landlords is now considerably less than *twenty-nine million pounds*. By far the larger part—namely something like *seventy million pounds* — is divided amongst *nine hundred and fifty thousand* owners, of whose stake in the country

figures with actual precision; but the returns in the New Doomsday Book, taken together with subsequent official information, enable us to arrive at the substantial facts of the case. In 1878 the rental of the owners of more than *a thousand* acres was *twenty-nine million pounds.* The rental of the rural owners of smaller estates was *thirty-two million pounds;* and the rental of small urban and suburban owners was *thirty-six million pounds.* The suburban properties averaged *three and a half* acres, the average rent being *thirteen pounds* per acre.

MULTITUDE OF SMALL LANDOWNERS 45

the agitator seems totally unaware; and in order to give to each man the above daily dividend, it would be necessary to rob all this immense multitude whose rentals are, on an average, *seventy-six pounds* a year.[1] Supposing, then, this nation of smaller landlords to

---

[1] According to the Local Government Report of 1878, the rental of all the properties over *five hundred* acres averaged *thirty-six shillings* an acre; that of properties between *fifty* and *a hundred* acres, *forty-eight shillings* an acre; and that of properties between *ten* and *fifty* acres, *a hundred and sixteen shillings* an acre. In Scotland, the rental of properties over *five hundred* acres averaged *nine shillings* an acre: that of properties between *ten* and *fifty* acres, *four hundred and thirteen shillings*. With regard to the value of properties under *ten* acres, the following Scotch statistics are interesting. Four-fifths of the ground rental of Edinburgh is taken by owners of less than one acre, the rental of such owners being on an average *ninety-nine pounds*. Three-fourths of the ground rental of Glasgow is taken by owners of similar plots of ground; only there the rental of such owners is *a hundred and seventy-one pounds*. In the municipal borough of Kilmarnock, land owned in plots of less than an acre lets per acre at *thirty-two pounds*. The land of the few men who own larger plots lets for not more than *twenty pounds*. Each one of the *eleven thousand* men who own collectively four-fifths of Edinburgh, has in point of money as much stake in the soil as though he were the owner in Sutherland of *two thousand* acres: and each one of the *ten thousand* men who own collectively three-fourths of Glasgow, has as much stake in the soil as though he were the owner in Sutherland of *three thousand four hundred* acres.

be spared, and our robbery confined to peers and to country gentlemen, the sum to be dealt with would be less than *twenty-nine million pounds*; and out of the ruin of every park, manor, and castle in the country, each adult male would receive less than three-farthings daily.

Marginalia: The entire rental of the landed aristocracy is so small that its confiscation would benefit no one.

And now let us turn to the National Debt and to the railways. The entire interest of the one and the entire profits of the other, would, if divided equally amongst the population, give results a little, but only a little, larger than the rental of the large landlords. But here again, if the poorer classes were spared, and the richer investors alone were singled out for attack, the small dividend of perhaps one penny for each man daily, would be diminished to a sum yet more insignificant. How true this is may be seen from the following figures relating to the National Debt. Out of the *two hundred and thirty-six thousand* persons who held consols in 1880, *two hundred and sixteen thousand*, or more than nine-tenths of the whole, derived from their investments less than *ninety pounds* a year; whilst nearly half of the whole derived less than *fifteen pounds*.

Marginalia: Were the National Debt and the Railways confiscated, the results would likewise be hardly perceptible to the nation as a whole.

And lastly, let us consider the Monarchy, with all its pomp and circumstance, the maintenance of which is constantly represented as a burden seriously pressing on the shoulders of the working-class. I am not arguing that in itself a Monarchy is better than a Republic. I am considering nothing but its cost in money to the nation. Let us see then what its maintenance actually costs each of us, and how much each of us might conceivably gain by its abolition. The total cost of the Monarchy is about *six hundred thousand pounds* a year; but ingenious Radicals have not infrequently argued that virtually, though indirectly, it costs as much as *a million pounds*. Let us take then this latter sum, and divide it amongst *thirty-eight million* people. What does it come to a head? It comes to something less than *sixpence halfpenny* a year. It costs each individual less to maintain the Queen than it would cost him to drink her health in a couple of pots of porter. The price of these pots is the utmost he could gain by the abolition of the Monarchy. But does any one think that the individual would gain so much—or indeed, gain any-

BOOK I.
CH. III.

The Monarchy costs so small a sum, that no one would be the richer for its abolition.

thing? If he does, he is singularly sanguine. Let him turn to countries that are under a Republican government; and he will find that elected Presidents are apt to cost more than Queens.

<small>All such schemes of redistribution are illusory, not only on account of the insignificance of their results,</small>

All these schemes, then, for attacking property as it exists, for confiscating and redistributing by some forcible process of legislation the whole or any part of the existing national income, are either obviously impracticable, or their result would be insignificant. Their utmost result indeed would not place any of the workers in so good a position as is at present occupied by many of them. This is evident from what has been seen already.

<small>But also on account of a far deeper reason, on which the whole problem depends.</small>

But there is another reason which renders such schemes illusory—a far more important one than any I have yet touched upon, and of a far more fundamental kind. We will consider this in the next chapter; and we shall find, when we have done so, that it has brought us to the real heart of the question.

CHAPTER IV

The Nature of the National Wealth: first, of the National Capital; second, of the National Income. Neither of these is susceptible of Arbitrary Division.

WE have just seen how disappointing, to those even who would gain most by it, would be the results of an equal division of the national income of this country, and how intolerable to all would be the general conditions involved in it. In doing this, we have of course adopted, for argument's sake, an assumption which underlies all popular ideas of such a process; namely, that if a Government were only strong enough and possessed the requisite will, it could deal with the national income in any way that might be desired; or, in other words, that the national income is something that could be divided and distributed, as an enormous heap

<small>A legislative division of the national income is not only disappointing in its theoretical results, but practically impossible,</small>

BOOK I.
CH. IV.

As will be shown in this chapter.

Wealth is utterly unlike money in its divisible qualities.

of sovereigns could, according to the will of any one who had them under his fingers. I am now going to show that this assumption is entirely false, and that even were it desirable theoretically that the national income should be redivided, it is not susceptible of any such arbitrary division.

To those who are unaccustomed to reflecting on economic problems, and who more or less consciously associate the qualities of wealth with those of the money in whose terms its amount is stated, I cannot introduce this important subject better than by calling their attention to the few following facts, which, simple and accessible as they are, are not generally known.

The capital value of the wealth of the United Kingdom is estimated at something like *ten thousand million pounds;* but the entire amount of sovereigns and shillings in the country does not exceed *a hundred and forty-four million pounds,* nor that of the uncoined bullion, *a hundred and twenty-two million pounds.* That is to say, for every nominal *ten thousand* sovereigns there does not exist in reality more than *two hundred* and twenty-six. Were this sum divided amongst the population equally, it would give every one a share of exactly *seven pounds.* Again, this country produces every year wealth which we express by calling it *thirteen hundred million pounds.* The amount of gold and silver produced annually by the whole world is hardly so much as *thirty-eight million pounds.* If the whole of this were appropriated by the United Kingdom, it would give annually to each inhabitant only ten new shillings and a single new half-sovereign. The United Kingdom, however, gets annually but a tenth of the world's money, so its annual share in reality is not so much as *four million pounds.* Accordingly, that vast volume of wealth which we express by calling it *thirteen hundred million pounds,* has but *four million pounds* of fresh money year by year to correspond to it. That is to say, there is only one new sovereign for every new nominal sum of *three hundred and twenty-five.*

Wealth as a whole, therefore, is something so totally distinct from money that there is no ground for presuming it to be divisible in the

The money of the United Kingdom is an imperceptible fraction of its wealth.

The nature of wealth, as a whole, is quite miscon-

same way. What is wealth, then, in a country like our own? To some people this will seem a superfluous question. They will say that every one knows what wealth is by experience —by the experience of possessing it, or by the experience of wanting it. And in a certain sense this is true, but not in any sense that concerns us here. In precisely the same sense every one knows what health is; but that is very different from knowing on what health depends; and to know the effects of wealth on our own existence is very different from knowing the nature of the thing that causes them. Indeed, as a matter of fact, what wealth really consists of is a thing which very few people are ever at the trouble to realise; and nothing shows that such is the case more clearly than the false and misleading images which are commonly used to represent it. The most familiar of these are: "a treasure," "a store," "a hoard," or, as the Americans say, "a pile." Now any one of these images is not only not literally true, but embodies and expresses a mischievous and misleading falsehood. It represents wealth as something which could be carried off and divided—as a kind of plunder which might be seized by a conquering army. But the truth is, that the amount of existing wealth which can be accurately described, or could be possibly treated in this way, is, in a country like ours, a very insignificant portion; and, were social conditions revolutionised to any serious degree, much of that portion would lose its value and cease to be wealth at all.

Let us take, for instance, some palatial house in London, which catches the public gaze as a monument of wealth and splendour; and we will suppose that a mob of five hundred people are incited to plunder it by a leader who informs them that its contents are worth *two hundred thousand pounds*. Assuming that estimate to be correct, would it mean that of these five hundred people each would get a portion to him worth *four hundred pounds?* Let us see what would really happen. They would find enough wine, perhaps, to keep them all drunk for a week; enough food to feed thirty of them for a day; and sheets and blankets for possibly thirty beds. But this would not account for many thousands out of the two hundred thousand pounds. The bulk of that sum would be made up — how? *A hundred thousand pounds* would be probably represented by some hundred and fifty pictures, and the rest by rare furniture, china, and works of art. Now all these things to the pillagers would be absolutely devoid of value; for if such pillage were general there would be nobody left to buy them; and they would in themselves give the pillagers no pleasure. One can imagine the feelings of a man who, expecting *four hundred pounds*, found himself presented with an unsaleable Sèvres broth-basin, or a picture of a Dutch burgomaster; or of five such men if for their share they were given a buhl cabinet between them. We may be quite certain that the broth-basin would be at once broken in anger; the cabinet would be tossed up for, and probably used as a rabbit-hutch; and the men as a body would endeavour to make up for their disappointment by ducking or lynching the leader who had managed to make such fools of them.

And now let us consider the wealth of the kingdom as a whole. Much as the bulk of it differs from the contents of a house of this kind, it would, if seized on in any forcible way, prove even more disappointing and elusive. {BOOK I. CH. IV. — susceptible of division.}

We may consider it under two aspects. We may consider it as so much annual income, or else as so much capital. In the last chapter we were considering it as so much income, and presently we shall be doing so again. But as capital may possibly strike the imagination of many as something more tangible and easily seized, and likely to yield, if redistributed, more satisfactory results, we will see first of what items the estimated capital of this country is composed. To do so will not only be instructive: it will also be curious and amusing. {Wealth, as a whole, has two aspects: that of capital, and that of income. We will first consider the national capital.}

As I said just now, its value, expressed in money, is according to the latest authorities about *ten thousand million pounds.*[1] As actual money, however, forms so minute a portion of this,—the reader will see that it is hardly more than one-fortieth,—we may, for {This capital consists not of money;}

---

[1] This is Mr. Giffen's estimate. Mr. Mulhall, who has made independent calculations, does not differ from Mr. Giffen by more than five per cent.

our present purpose, pass it entirely over; and our concern will be solely with the things for which our millions are a mere expression.

Butofthree classes of things: the two first comprising things not susceptible of division;

It will be found that these things divide themselves into three classes. The first consists of things which, from their very nature, are not susceptible of any forcible division at all; the second consists of things which are susceptible of division only by a process of physically destroying them and pulling them into pieces; and each of these two classes, in point of value, represents, roughly speaking, nearly a quarter of the total. The third class alone, which represents little more than a half, consists of things which, even theoretically, could be divided without being destroyed.

The third class comprising all those things that could be divided without destroying them; and forming about half of the total.

We will consider this third class first, which represents in the estimates of statisticians *five thousand seven hundred million pounds.* The principal things comprised in it are land, houses, furniture, works of art, clothing, merchandise, provisions, and live-stock; and such commodities in general as change hands over the shopman's counter, or in the market.[1]

[1] General merchandise is estimated by Mr. Mulhall at

Of these items, by far the largest is houses, which make up a quarter of the capital value of the country, or *two thousand five hundred million pounds*. But more than half this sum stands for houses which are much above the average in size, and which do not form more than an eighth part of the whole; and were they apportioned to a new class of occupants, they would lose at least three-fourths of their present estimated value. So too with regard to furniture and works of art, a large part of their estimated value would, as we have seen already, disappear in distribution likewise: and their estimated value is about a tenth of the whole we are now considering. Land, of course, can, at all events in theory, be divided with far greater

three hundred and forty-three million pounds. For every *hundred* inhabitants in the year 1877 there were *five* horses, *twenty-eight* cows, *seventy-six* sheep, and *ten* pigs. In 1881 there were in Great Britain *five million four hundred and seventy-five thousand* houses. The rent of eighty-seven per cent of these was under *thirty pounds* a year, and the rental of more than a half averaged only *ten pounds*. The total house-rental of Great Britain in that year was *one hundred and fourteen million pounds;* and the aggregate total of houses over *thirty pounds* annual value was *sixty million pounds;* though in point of number these houses were only thirteen per cent of the whole.

BOOK I.
CH. IV.

advantage; and counts in the estimates as *fifteen hundred million pounds*—or something under a sixth of the whole. Merchandise, provisions, and movable goods in general can be divided yet more readily; and so one would think could live-stock, though this is hardly so in reality: but of the whole these three last items form little more than a twentieth.

The results of dividing these would be ridiculous.

And now, supposing all these divisible things to be divided, let us see what the capital would look like which would be allotted to each individual. Each individual would find himself possessed of a lodging of some sort, together with clothes and furniture worth about *eight pounds*. He would have about *eight pounds'* worth of provisions and miscellaneous movables, and a ring, a pin, or a brooch, worth about *three pounds ten shillings*. He would also be the proprietor of one acre of land, which would necessarily in many cases be miles away from his dwelling, whilst as to stocking his acre, he would be met by the following difficulty. He would find himself entitled to the twentieth part of a horse, to two-thirds of a sheep, the fourth part of a cow, and the tenth part of a pig.

Such then would be the result to the individual of dividing the whole of our capital that could be divided without destroying it. This is, as we said, a little more than half of the total; and now let us turn to the two other quarters; beginning with the things which could be indeed divided, but which would obviously be destroyed in the process. Their estimated value is more than *two thousand million pounds:* half of which sum is represented by the railways and shipping of the kingdom; *six hundred million pounds*, by gasworks and the machinery in our factories; and the rest, by roads and streets and public works and buildings. These, it is obvious, are not suitable for division; and still less divisible are the things in the class that still remains. For of their total value, which amounts to some *two thousand five hundred million pounds*, more than *a thousand million pounds*, according to Mr. Giffen, represent the good-will of various professions of business; and the whole of the remainder—nearly *fifteen hundred million*

BOOK I.
CH. IV.

The second class of things, comprising the national capital, could not be divided without destroying them.

The remaining class of things could not be divided at all.

BOOK I.
CH. IV.

pounds—represents nothing that is in the United Kingdom at all, but merely legal claims on the part of particular British subjects to a share in the proceeds of enterprise in other countries.

This last class consists of things which are merely rights and advantages secured by law, and dependent on existing social conditions; and it can be easily understood how they would disappear under any attempt to seize them. But the remaining three quarters of our capital consists of material things; and what we have seen with regard to them may strike many people as incredible; for the moment we imagine them violently seized and distributed, they seem to dwindle and shrivel up; and the share of each individual suggests to one's mind nothing but a series of ludicrous pictures—pictures of men whose heritage in all this unimaginable wealth is an acre of ground, two wheels of a steam-engine, a bedroom, a pearl pin, and the tenth part of a pig.

Capital has no value at all, except when vivified by use;

The explanation, however, of this result is to be found in the recognition of an exceedingly simple fact: that the capital of a country is of hardly any value at all, and is, as capital, of no value at all, when regarded merely as an aggregate of material things, and not as material things made living by their connection with life. The land, which is worth *fifteen hundred million pounds*, depends for its value on the application of human labour to it, and the profitable application of labour depends on skill and intelligence. The value of the houses depends on our means of living in them—depends not on themselves, but on the way in which they are inhabited. What are railways or steamships, regarded as dead matter, or all the machinery belonging to all the manufacturing companies? Nothing. They are no more wealth than a decomposing corpse is a man. They become wealth only when life fills them with movement by a power which, like all vital processes, is one of infinite complexity: when multitudes are massed in this or in that spot, or diffused sparsely over this or that district; when trains move at appropriate seasons, and coal finds its way from the mine to the engine-furnace. The only parts of the capital in existence at any given moment, which deserve the name of capital as mere material things, are the stores of food, fuel, and clothing existing in granaries, shops, and elsewhere; and not only is the value of these proportionately small, but, if not renewed constantly, they would in a few weeks be exhausted.

And it obviously cannot be used if it is equally distributed.

It is plain then that, under the complicated system of production to which the wealth of the modern world is due, an equal division of the capital of a country like our own is not the way to secure an equal division of wealth. The only thing that could conceivably be divided is income. If, however, it is true that capital is, as we have seen it is, in its very nature living, and ceases to be itself the moment that life goes out of it, still more emphatically must the same thing be said of income, for the sake of producing which capital is alone accumulated. Agitators talk of the national income as if it were a dead tree which a statesman like Mr. Gladstone could cut into chips and distribute. It is not like a dead tree; it is like the living column of a fountain, of which every particle is in constant movement, and of which the substance is never for two minutes the same.

Income is all that could conceivably be thus divided.

ALONE WORTH CONSIDERING

Let us examine the details of this income, and the truth of what has been said will be apparent. The total amount, as we have seen, is estimated at *thirteen hundred million pounds;* it is not, however, made up of sovereigns, but of things of which sovereigns are nothing more than the measure. The true income of the nation and the true income of the individual consist alike of things which are actually consumed or enjoyed; or of legal rights to such things which are accumulated for future exercise. Of these last, which, in other words, are savings, and are estimated to amount to *a hundred and thirty million pounds* annually, we need not speak here, except to deduct them from the total spent. The total is thus reduced to *eleven hundred and seventy million pounds*—or to things actually consumed or enjoyed, which are valued at that figure. Now what are these things? That is our present question. By far the larger part of them comes under the following heads: Food, Clothing, Lodging, Fuel and Lighting, the attendance of Servants, the Defence of the Country and Empire, and the Maintenance of Law and Order. These together represent

BOOK I.
CH. IV.

The national income consists of money no more than the national capital does. It consists of other things, or rights to other things; Namely, of perishable goods, durable goods, and services.

about *eight hundred million pounds*. Of the remaining *three hundred and seventy million pounds*, about a third is represented by the transport of goods and travelling; and not much more than a quarter of the total income, or about *two hundred and seventy million pounds*, by new furniture, pictures, books, plate, and other miscellaneous articles. The furniture produced annually counts for something like *forty million pounds;* and the new plate for not more than *five hundred thousand pounds.*

And now let us examine these things from certain different points of view, and see how in each case they group themselves into different classes.

In the first place, they may be classified thus: into things that are wealth because they are consumed, things that are wealth because they are owned, and things that are wealth because they are used or occupied. Under the first heading come food, clothing, lighting, and fuel; under the second, movable chattels; and under the third, the occupation of houses,[1] the services of domestics, the

[1] This classification of houses may perhaps be objected to;

carrying of letters by the Post Office, transport and travelling, and the defences and administration of the country. In other words, the first class consists of new perishable goods, the second of new durable goods, and the third not of goods at all, but of services and uses. The relative amounts of value of the three will be shown with sufficient accuracy by the following rough estimates.

Of a total of *eleven hundred and seventy million pounds*, perishable goods count for *five hundred and twenty million pounds*, durable goods and chattels for *two hundred*

but from the above point of view it is correct. Houses represent an annual income of *one hundred and thirty-five million pounds*. Not more than *thirty-five million pounds* are spent annually in building new houses; whilst the whole are counted as representing a new *one hundred million pounds* every year. It is plain, therefore, that if we estimate the entire annual value as above, the sum in question stands not for the houses, but for the use of them. Even more clearly does the same reasoning apply to railways and shipping. Whether we send goods by these or are conveyed by them ourselves, all that we get from them is the mere service of transport. On transport and travelling by railway about *seventy million pounds* are spent annually: by ship about *thirty million pounds;* by trams about *two million pounds.*

BOOK I.
CH. IV.

and fifty million pounds, and services and uses for *four hundred million pounds*. Thus, less than a quarter of what we call the national income consists of material things which we can keep and collect about us; little less than half consists of material things which are only produced to perish, and perish almost as fast as they are made; and more than a third consists of actions and services which are not material at all, and pass away and renew themselves even faster than food and fuel.

A large part of the national income consists of things that are imported.

This is how the national income appears, as seen from one point of view. Let us change our ground, and see how it appears to us from another. We shall see the uses and the services—to the value of *four hundred million pounds*—still grouped apart as before. But the remaining elements, representing nearly *eight hundred million pounds*, and consisting of durable and perishable material things, we shall see dividing itself in an entirely new way — into material things made at home, and material things imported. We shall see that the imported things come to very nearly half;[1] and we shall see further that

[1] The total annual imports are about *four hundred and*

amongst these imported things food forms incomparably the largest item. But the significance of this fact is not fully apparent till we consider what is the total amount of food consumed by us; and when we do that, we shall see that, exclusive of alcoholic drinks, actually more than half come to us from other countries.[1] The reader perhaps may think that this imported portion consists largely of luxuries, which, on occasion, we could do without. If he does think so, let him confine his attention to those articles which are most necessary, and most universally consumed—namely bread, meat, tea, coffee, and sugar—and he will see that our imports are to our home produce as *ninety* to *seventy-three*. If we strike out the last three, our position is still more startling;[2] and most startling if

Most of our food is imported.

---

twenty million pounds. The amount retained for home consumption is about *three hundred and sixty-five million pounds.*

[1] The approximate value of the food consumed annually in the United Kingdom (exclusive of alcoholic drinks) is *two hundred and ninety million pounds.* The total value of food imported is over *one hundred and fifty million pounds.*

[2] The number of persons fed on home-grown meat was *twenty-three millions one hundred thousand.* The number fed on imported meat was *fourteen millions seven hundred thousand.*

we confine ourselves to the prime necessary—bread. The imported wheat is to the home-grown wheat as *twenty-six* to *twelve*: that is to say, of the population of this kingdom *twenty-six millions* subsist on wheat that is imported, and only *twelve millions* on wheat that is grown at home; or, to put the matter in a slightly different way, we all subsist on imported wheat for eight months of the year.

And now let the reader reflect on what all this means. It means that of the material part of the national income half consists, not of goods which we ourselves produce, but of foreign goods which are exchanged for them; and are exchanged for them only because, by means of the most far-reaching knowledge, and the most delicate adaptation of skill, we are able to produce goods fitted to the wants and tastes of distant nations and communities, many of which are to most of us hardly even known by name. On every workman's breakfast-table is a meeting of all the continents and of all the zones;

Thus the national income is a product of infinite complexity.

In other words, the number of persons who subsist on imported meat now is about equal to the entire population of the United Kingdom in 1801.

and they are united there by a thousand processes that never pause for a moment, and thoughts and energies that never for a moment sleep.

A consideration of these facts will be enough to bring home to anybody the accuracy of the simile of which I made use just now, when I compared the income of the nation to the column thrown up by a fountain. He will see how, like such a column, it is a constant stream of particles, taking its motion from a variety of complicated forces, and how it is a phenomenon of force quite as much as a phenomenon of matter. He will see that it is a living thing, not a dead thing: and that it can no more be distributed by any mechanical division of it, than the labour of a man can be distributed by cutting his limbs to pieces.

This simile of the fountain, though accurate, is, like most similes, incomplete. It will, however, serve to introduce us to one peculiarity more by which our national income is distinguished, and which has an even greater significance than any we have yet dealt with.

In figuring the national income as the water thrown up by a fountain, we of course suppose

Its amount also varies owing to infinitely complicated causes,

BOOK I.
CH. IV.

its estimated amount or value to be represented by the volume of the water and the height to which it is thrown. What I am anxious now to impress on the attention of the reader is that the height and volume of our national fountain of riches are never quite the same from one year to another; whilst we need not extend our view beyond the limits of one generation to see that they have varied in the most astonishing manner. The height and volume of the fountain are now very nearly double what they were when Mr. Gladstone was in Lord Aberdeen's Ministry.[1]

Which are quite independent of the growth of population;

Some readers will perhaps be tempted to say that in this there is nothing wonderful, for it is due to the increase of population. But the increase of population has nothing to do with the matter. It cannot have anything to do with what I am now stating. For when I say that within a certain period the income of the nation has doubled itself, I mean that it has doubled itself in proportion to the population; so that, no matter how many more

---

[1] From the year 1843 to 1851, the annual income of the nation averaged *five hundred and fifteen million pounds*, according to the calculations of Messrs. Leone Levi, Dudley Baxter, Mulhall, and Giffen.

millions of people there may be in the country now than there were at the beginning of the period in question, there is annually produced for each million of people now nearly twice the income that was produced for each million of people then. Or in other words, an equal division now would give each man nearly double the amount that it would have given him when Mr. Gladstone was beginning to be middle-aged.

But we must not be content with comparing our national income with itself. Let us compare it also with the incomes of other countries; and let it in all cases be understood that the comparison is between the income as related to the respective populations, and not between the absolute totals. We will begin with France. It is estimated that, within the last hundred and ten years, the income of France has, relatively to the population, increased more than fourfold. A division of the income in 1780 would have given *six pounds* a head to everybody : a similar division now would give everybody *twenty-seven pounds*. And yet the income of France, after all this rapid growth, is to-day twenty-one per cent less than that

As we may see by comparing the income of this country with the income of others.

of the United Kingdom. Other comparisons we shall find even more striking. Relatively to the respective populations, the income of the United Kingdom exceeds that of Norway in the proportion of *thirty-four* to *twenty;* that of Switzerland, in the proportion of *thirty-four* to *nineteen;* that of Italy, in the proportion of *thirty-four* to *twelve;* and that of Russia, in the proportion of *thirty-four* to *eleven.* The comparison with Italy and Russia brings to light a remarkable fact. Were all the property of the upper classes in those countries confiscated, and the entire incomes distributed in equal shares, the share of each Russian would be fifty per cent less, and of each Italian forty per cent less than what each inhabitant of the United Kingdom would receive from a division of the income of its wage-earning classes only.

We find, therefore, that if we take equal populations of men,—populations, let us say, of a million men each,—either belonging to the same nation at different dates, or to different civilised nations at the same date, that the incomes produced by no two of them reach to the same amount; but that, on the contrary, the differences between the largest income and the others range from twenty to two hundred per cent.

BOOK I.
CH. IV.

Now what is the reason of this? Perhaps it will be said that differences of race are the reason. That may explain a little, but it will not explain much; for these differences between the incomes produced by equal bodies of men are not observable only when men are of different races; but the most striking examples, —namely, those afforded by our own country and France—are differences between the incomes produced by the same race during different decades—by the same race, and by many of the same individuals.

The causes of these differences in income are not differences of race,

Perhaps then it will be said that they are due to differences of soil and climate. But again, that will not explain the differences, at various dates, between the incomes of the same countries; and though it may explain a little, it will not explain much, of the differences at the same date between the incomes of different countries. The soil and climate, for instance, of the United Kingdom, are not in themselves more suited for agriculture than the soil and climate of France and Belgium; and yet for

Nor of soil or climate,

BOOK I. CH. IV.

each individual actually engaged in agriculture, this country produces in value twenty-five per cent more than France, and forty per cent more than Belgium. I may add that it produces forty-six per cent more than Germany, sixty-six per cent more than Austria, and sixty per cent more than Italy.[1]

Nor of hours of labour,

Perhaps then a third explanation will be suggested. These differences will be said to be due to differences in the hours of labour. But a moment's consideration will show that that has nothing to do with the problem; for when a million people in this country produced half what they produce to-day, they had fewer holidays, and they worked longer hours. Now that they have doubled the annual produce, they take practically four weeks less in producing it.[2] Again, the hours of labour for the manufacturing classes are in Switzerland

[1] The actual figures are as follows:—In 1887 the estimates of the value of agricultural products per each individual actually engaged in agriculture were : United Kingdom, *ninety-eight pounds* ; France, *seventy - one pounds* ; Belgium, *fifty - six pounds* ; Germany, *fifty - two pounds* ; Austria, *thirty - one pounds*; Italy, *thirty-seven pounds.*

[2] It is understating the case to say that the British operative to-day works one hundred and eighty-nine hours less annually than his predecessor of forty or fifty years ago,

twenty-six per cent longer at the present time than in this country; and yet the annual product, in proportion to the number of operatives, is twenty-eight per cent less.[1]

Agriculture gives us examples of the same discrepancy between the labour expended and the value of the result obtained. In France, the agricultural population is three times what it is in this country, but the value of the agricultural produce is not so much as double.[2]

Plainly, therefore, the growth of a nation's income, under modern conditions, does not depend on an increased expenditure of labour. There might, indeed, seem some ground for leaping to the contrary conclusion—that it grows in proportion as the hours of labour are limited: but whatever incidental truth there

and one hundred and eighty-nine hours = three weeks of nine hours a day. To this must be added at least a week of additional holidays.

[1] The hours of labour in Switzerland are, on an average, sixty-six a week.

[2] The agricultural population in France is about *eighteen millions;* in this country, about *six millions.* The produce of France is worth about *four hundred and fourteen million pounds;* of this country, *two hundred and twenty-six million pounds.*

BOOK I. CH. IV.

But are causes of some other kind which lie below the surface,

may be in that contention, it does not explain the main facts we are dealing with; for some of the most rapid changes in the incomes of nations we find have occurred during periods when the hours of labour remained unaltered; and we find at the present moment that countries in which the hours of labour are the same, differ even more, in point of income, from one another than they differ from countries in which the hours of labour are different. Whatever, therefore, the causes of such differences may be, they are not simple and superficial causes like these.

I have alluded to the incomes of foreign countries only for the sake of throwing more light on the income of our own. Let us again turn to that. Half of that income, as we have seen, consists to-day of an annual product new since the time when men still in their prime were children; and this mysterious addition to our wealth has rapidly and silently developed itself, without one person in a thousand being aware of its extent, or realising the operation of any new forces that might account for it. Let people of middle age look back to their own childhood; and the England of that time, in aspects and modes of life, will not seem to them very different from what it seems now. Let them turn over a book of John Leech's sketches, which appeared in *Punch* about the time of the first Exhibition; and, putting aside a few changes in feminine fashion, they will see a faithful representation of the life that still surrounds them. The street, the drawing-room, the hunting-field, the railway-station—nothing will be obsolete, nothing out-of-date. Nothing will suggest that since these sketches were made any perceptible change has come over the conditions of our civilisation. And yet, somehow or other, some changes have taken place, owing to which our income has nearly doubled itself. In other words, the existence of one-half of our wealth is due to causes, the nature, the presence, and the operation of which, are hidden so completely beneath the surface of life as to escape altogether the eye of ordinary observation, and reveal themselves only to careful and deliberate search.

The practical moral of all this is obvious: that just as our income has doubled itself

BOOK I.
CH. IV.

And which requires to be carefully searched for.

For, unless we understand the

Causes which have made our national income grow, we may, by interfering with them unknowingly, make our income decrease: without our being aware of the causes, and almost without our being aware of the fact, so unless we learn what the causes are, and are consequently able to secure for them fair play, or, at all events, to avoid interfering with their operation, we may lose what we have gained even more quickly than we have gained it, and annihilate the larger part of what we are desirous to distribute. We have seen that the national income is a living thing; and, as is the case with other living things, the principles of its growth reside in parts of the body which are themselves not sensitive to pain, but which may for the moment be deranged and injured with impunity, and will betray their injury only by results which arise afterwards, and which may not be perceived till it is too late to remedy them.

And this is the danger of reckless social legislation. Here lies the danger of reckless social legislation, and even of the reckless formation of vague public opinion; for public opinion, in a democratic country like ours, is legislation in its nebular stage: and hence the only way to avert this danger is, first to do what we have just now been doing,—to consider the amount and character of the wealth with which we have to deal, — and secondly, to examine the causes to which the production of this wealth has been due, and on which the maintenance of its continued production must depend.

{BOOK I. CH. IV.}

Let the social reformer lay the following reflections to his heart. Some of the more ardent and hopeful of the leaders of the labour-party to-day imagine that considerable changes in the distribution of the national income may be brought about by the close of the present century. In other words, they prophesy that the Government will seven years hence do certain things with that year's national income. But the national income of that year is not yet in existence; and what grounds have those sanguine persons for thinking that when it is produced it will be as large, or even half as large, as the national income is to-day? What grounds have they for believing that, if the working-classes then take everything, they will be as rich as they are now when they take only a part? The only ground on which such a belief can be justified is the implied belief that the same conditions and forces which have swelled the

{We will therefore, in the following Book, examine what these causes are.}

national income to its present vast amount, will still continue in undisturbed operation.

We will now proceed to consider what these conditions and forces are.

BOOK II

THE CHIEF FACTOR IN THE PRODUCTION
OF THE NATIONAL INCOME

CHAPTER I

Of the various Factors in Production, and how to distinguish the Amount produced by each.

THE inquiry on which we are entering really comprises two. I will explain how.

Although, as we have seen, of the yearly income of the nation a part only consists of material things, yet the remainder depends upon these, and its amount is necessarily in proportion to them. Accordingly, when we are dealing with the question of how the income is produced, we may represent the whole of it as a great heap of commodities, which every year disappears, and is every year replaced by a new one. Here then we have a heap of commodities on one side, and on the other the subjects of our inquiry—namely, the conditions and forces which produce that heap.

Now, as to what these conditions and forces

> BOOK II. CH. I.
>
> Land, Capital, and Human Exertion are the three factors in production; but at present we may omit Capital.

are, there is a familiar answer ready for us—Land, Labour, and Capital; and, with a certain reservation, we may take this to be true. But as Capital is itself the result of Land and Labour, we need not, for the moment, treat Capital separately; but we may say that the heap is produced by Land and Labour simply. I use this formula, however, only for the purpose of amending it. It will be better, for reasons with which I shall deal presently, instead of the term Labour to use the term Human Exertion. And further, we must remember this—the heap of commodities we have in view is no mere abstraction, but represents the income of this country at some definite date; so that when we are talking of the forces and conditions that have produced it, we mean not only Human Exertion and Land, but Human Exertion of a certain definite amount applied to Land of a definite extent and quality.

> The first point we notice is that the exertion of the same number of men applied to

Now, as I pointed out in the last Book, one of the most remarkable things about our national production of commodities, is that the yearly exertion of the same number of men, applied to land of the same extent and quality, has been far from producing always a heap of

THE PRODUCTION OF GIVEN QUANTITIES 85

the same size. On the contrary, the heap which it produces to-day is twice as large as that which it produced in the days of our fathers; and nearly three times as large as that which it produced in the days of our grandfathers. Here then is the reason why the inquiry that is before us is twofold. For we have at first to take some one of such heaps singly—on several accounts it will be convenient to take the smallest, namely that produced about a hundred years ago—and to analyse the parts which Land and Human Exertion played respectively in the production of *it*. Then, having seen how Land and Human Exertion produced in the days of our grandfathers a heap of this special size, we must proceed to inquire why three generations later the same land and the exertions of a similar number of men produce a heap which is nearly three times as large. For the difference of result cannot be due to nothing. It must be due to some difference in one of the two causes—to the presence in this cause of some varying element: and it is precisely here —here in this varying element—that the main interest of our inquiry centres. For if it is

BOOK II. CH. I.

the same land does not always produce the same amount of wealth.

This must be due to some varying element in the Human Exertion in question.

owing to a variation in this element that our productive powers have nearly trebled themselves in the course of three generations, nearly two-thirds of the income which the nation enjoys at present depends on the present condition of this element being maintained, and not being suffered—as it very easily might be—to again become what it was three generations back. Let us begin then with taking the amount of commodities produced in this country at the end of the last century, which is at once the most convenient and the most natural period to select; for production was then entering on its present stage of development, and its course from then till now is more or less familiar to us all.

Let us compare production in this country 100 years ago with production now.

We will start therefore with the fact that, about a hundred years ago, our national income, if divided equally amongst the inhabitants of the kingdom, would have yielded to each inhabitant a share of about *fourteen pounds;* so that if we confine ourselves to Great Britain, the population of which was then about *ten millions*, we have a national income of *a hundred and forty million pounds*, or a heap of commodities produced every year to an amount that is indicated by that money value. Let us take then any one of the closing years of the last century, and consider for a moment the causes at work in this island to which the production of such a heap of commodities was due.

In general language, these causes have been described already as Human Exertion of a certain definite amount applied to Land of a certain definite extent and quality; but it will now be well to restore to its traditional place the accumulated result of past exertion—namely Capital, and to think of it as a separate cause, according to the usual practice. For everybody knows that at the close of the last century, many sorts of machinery, and stores of all sorts of necessaries, were made and accumulated to assist and maintain Labour; and it is of such things that Capital principally consists. The Capital of Great Britain was at that time about *sixteen hundred million pounds*.[1] We will accordingly say that about a hundred years ago, the Land of this island, the Capital of this island, and the Exertions of

[1] According to Eden it was about *seventeen hundred million pounds* at the beginning of the present century. Twenty-five years previously it was, according to Young's estimate, *eleven hundred million pounds*.

a population of *ten million* people produced together, every twelve months, a heap of commodities worth *a hundred and forty million pounds*. We need not, however, dwell, till later, on these details. For the present our national production at this particular period may be taken to represent the production of wealth generally.

How much in each case did Land, Capital, and Human Exertion produce respectively?

Now the question, let it be remembered, with which we are concerned ultimately, is how wealth, as produced in the modern world, may be distributed. Accordingly, since the distribution of it presupposes its production, and since we are agreed generally as to what the causes of its production are,—namely, Land, Capital, and Human Exertion,—our next great step is to inquire what proportion of the product is to be set down as due to each of these causes separately; for it is by this means only that we can see how and to what extent our social arrangements may be changed, without our production being diminished. And I cannot introduce the subject in a better way than by quoting the following passage from John Stuart Mill, in which he declares such an inquiry to be both meaningless and impossible to answer; for that it *can* be answered, and that it is full of meaning, and that to ask and answer it is a practical and fundamental necessity, will be made all the plainer by the absurdity of Mill's denial.

"Some writers," he says, "have raised the question whether Nature (or, in the language of economics, Land) gives more assistance to Labour in one kind of industry or another, and have said that in some occupations Labour does most; in others, Nature most. In this, however, there seems much confusion of ideas. The part which Nature has in any work of man is indefinite and immeasurable. It is impossible to decide that in any one thing Nature does more than in any other. One cannot even say that Labour does less. Less Labour may be required; but if that which is required is absolutely indispensable, the result is just as much the product of Labour as of Nature. When two conditions are equally necessary for producing the effect at all, it is unmeaning to say that so much of it is produced by one and so much by the other. It is like attempting to decide which half of a pair of scissors has most to do with the act of

Mill declares this question to be meaningless;

cutting; or, which of the factors—five or six—has most to do with the production of thirty." So writes Mill in the first chapter of his *Principles of Political Economy*; and if what he says is true with regard to Land and Labour (or, as we are calling it, Human Exertion), it is equally true with regard to Human Exertion and Capital; for without Human Exertion, Capital could produce nothing, and without Capital modern industry would be impossible: and thus, according to Mill's argument, we cannot assign to either of them a specific portion of the product. But Mill's argument is altogether unsound; and the actual facts of life, and a large part of Mill's own book, little as he perceived that it was so, are virtually a complete refutation of it.

To understand this, the reader need only reflect on those three principal and familiar parts into which the annual income of every civilised nation is divided, not only in actual practice, but theoretically by Mill himself—namely Rent, Interest, and Wages.[1] For

---

[1] I have not mentioned Profits. They consist, says Mill, of Interest, or Capital, and Wages, or Superintendence; to which he adds compensation for risk—a most important item, but not requiring to be included here.

these—what are they? The answer is very simple. They are portions of the income which correspond, at all events in theory, to the amounts produced respectively by Land, Capital, and Human Exertion; and which are on that account distributed amongst three sets of men—those who own the Land, those who own the Capital, and those who have contributed the Exertion. There are many causes which in practice may prevent the correspondence being complete; but that the general way in which the income is actually distributed is based on the amount produced by these three things respectively,—Land, Capital, and Human Exertion,—is a fact which no one can doubt who has once taken the trouble to consider it. It is thus perfectly clear that, contrary to what Mill says, though two or more agencies may be equally indispensable to the production of any wealth at all, it is not only not "unmeaning to say that so much is produced by one and so much by the other," but it is possible to make the calculation with practical certainty and precision; and I will now proceed to explain the principles on which it is made.

CHAPTER II

How the Product of Land is to be distinguished from the Product of Human Exertion.

THE question before us will be most easily understood if we begin with once again waiving any consideration of Capital, and if we deal only with what Mill, in the passage just quoted, calls "Nature and Labour"—or, in other words, with Land and Human Exertion. We will also, for simplicity's sake, confine ourselves to one use of land—its primary and most important use, namely its use in agriculture or food-production.

Rent is the proportion of the produce produced not by Human Exertion, but by the Land itself;

Now a British tenant-farmer who lives solely by his farming obviously derives his whole income from the produce of the soil he occupies; but the whole of this produce does not go to himself. Part is paid away in the form of rent to his landlord, and part in the form of wages to his labourers. We may however suppose, without altering the situation, that he has no labourers under him—that he is his own labourer as well as his own manager, and that the whole of the produce that is not set aside as rent goes to himself as the wages of his own exertion. The point on which I am going to insist is this—that whilst the exertion has produced the product that is taken as wages, the soil—or to speak more accurately—a certain quality in the soil has just as truly produced the produce that goes in rent—in fact that "Nature and Labour, though equally necessary for producing the effect at all," each produce respectively a certain definite part of it.

In order to prove this it will be enough to make really clear to the reader the explanation of rent which is given by all economists—an explanation in which men of the most opposite schools agree—men like Ricardo, and men like Mr. Henry George; and of which Mill himself is one of the most illustrious exponents. I shall myself attempt to add nothing new to it, except a greater simplicity of statement and illustration, and a special

BOOK II. CH. II.

As will be shown in this chapter by reference to the universally accepted theory of Rent.

stress on a certain part of its meaning, the importance of which has been hitherto disregarded.

Now, as we are going to take the industry of agriculture for our example, we shall mean by rent a portion of the agricultural products derived from Human Exertion applied to a given tract of soil. Of such products let us take corn, and use it, for simplicity's sake, as representing all the rest; and that being settled, let us go yet a step further; and, for simplicity's sake also, let us represent corn by bread; and imagine that loaves develop themselves in the soil like potatoes, and, when the ground is properly tilled, are dug up ready for consumption. We shall figure rent therefore as a certain number of loaves that are dug up from a given tract of soil. Now everybody knows that all soils are not equally good. That there is good land and that there is poor land is a fact quite familiar even to people who have never spent a single day in the country. And this means, if we continue the above supposition, that different fields of precisely the same size, cultivated by similar men and with the same expenditure of exertion, will yield to their respective cultivators different numbers of loaves.

Let us take an example. Tom, Dick, and Harry, we will say, are three brothers, who have each inherited a field of twelve acres. They are all equally strong, and equally industrious: we may suppose, in fact, that they all came into the world together, and are as like one another as three Enfield rifles. Each works in his field for the same time every day, digs up as many loaves as he can, and every evening brings them home in a basket. But when they come to compare the number that has been dug up by each, Tom always finds that he has fifteen loaves, Dick that he has twelve, and Harry that he has only nine; the reason being that in the field owned by Harry fewer loaves develop themselves than in the fields owned by Tom and Dick. Harry digs up fewer, because there are fewer to dig up. Let us consider Harry's case first.

Each of the loaves is, we will say, worth fourpence; therefore Harry, with his nine loaves, makes three shillings a day, or eighteen shillings a week. This is just enough to support him, according to the ideas and habits

We will illustrate this by the case of three men of equal power tilling three fields of unequal fertility.

Labour must be held to produce so much as is absolutely necessary for its own support.

of his class. If his field were such that it yielded him fewer loaves, or if he had to give even one of the loaves away, the field would be useless; it would not be cultivated at all, either by him, or by anybody, nor could it be; for the entire produce, which would then go to the cultivator, would not be enough to induce, or perhaps even to make him able, to cultivate it. But, as matters stand, so long as the entire produce does go to him, and to no one else, we must take it for granted that his exertion and his field between them yield him a livelihood which, according to his habits, is sufficient; for otherwise, as I have said, this field neither would nor could be cultivated. And it will be well here to make the general observation that whenever we find a class of men cultivating the utmost area of land which their strength permits, and taking for themselves the entire produce, their condition offers the highest standard of living that can possibly be general amongst peasant cultivators: from which it follows that, unless no land is cultivated except the best, the general standard of living must necessarily require less than the entire produce which the best land will yield. We assume then that Harry, with his nine loaves a day, represents the highest standard of living that is, or that can be, general amongst his class.

And now let us turn from Harry's case to the case of Tom and Dick. They have been accustomed to precisely the same standard of living as he has been; and they require for their support precisely the same amount of produce. But each day, after they have all of them fared alike, each taking the same quantity from his own particular basket, the baskets of Tom and Dick present a different appearance to that of Harry. There is in each of the two first a something which is not to be found in his. There is a surplus. In Dick's basket there are three extra loaves remaining; and in Tom's basket there are six. To what then is the production of these extra loaves due? Is it due to land, or is it due to the exertions of Tom and Dick? Mill, as we have seen, would tell us that this was an unmeaning question; but we shall soon see that it is not so.

It is perfectly true that it would be an unmeaning question if we had to do with one of the brothers only—say with Harry, and only with Harry's field. Then, no doubt, it would be impossible to say which produced most—Harry or the furrows tilled by him,—whether Harry produced two loaves and the furrows seven, or Harry seven and the furrows two. And to Harry's case more must be said than this. Such a calculation with regard to it would be not only impossible, but useless; for even if we convinced ourselves that the land produced seven loaves, and Harry's exertion only two, all the loaves would still of necessity go to Harry. In a case like this, therefore, it is quite sufficient to take account of Human Exertion only. Agricultural labour, in fact, must be held to produce whatever product is necessary for the customary maintenance of the labourer. But if this is the entire product obtained from the worst soil cultivated, it cannot be the entire product obtained from the best soil; and the moment we have to deal with a second field,—a field which is of a different quality, and which, although it is of exactly the same size, and is cultivated every day with precisely similar labour, yields to that labour a larger number of loaves,—twelve loaves, or fifteen loaves,

But whatever is beyond this is the product not of Labour, but of Land;

instead of nine,—then our position altogether changes. We are not only able, but obliged to consider Land as well as Labour, and to discriminate between their respective products. A calculation which was before as unmeaning as Mill declares it to be, not only becomes intelligible, but is forced on us.

For if we start with the generalisation derived from Harry's case, or any other case in which the land is of a similar quality that one man's labour produces nine loaves daily, and then find that Tom and Dick, for the same amount of labour, are rewarded respectively by fifteen loaves or by twelve, we have six extra loaves in one case, and three in the other, which cannot have been produced by Labour, and which yet must have been produced by something. They cannot have been produced by Labour; for the very assumption with which we start is that the Labour is the same in the last two cases as in the first; and according to all common-sense and all logical reasoning, the same cause cannot produce two different results. When results differ, the cause of the difference must be sought in some cause that varies, not a cause that remains the same;

As we shall see by comparing the case of the man tilling the best field with that of the man tilling the worst.

and the only cause that here varies is the Land. Accordingly, just as in Harry's case we are neither able nor concerned to credit the Land with any special part, or indeed any part, of the product, but say that all the nine loaves are produced by Harry's Labour, so too in the case of Tom and Dick we credit Labour with a precisely similar number; but all loaves beyond that number we credit not to their Labour, but to their Land—or, to speak more accurately, to certain qualities which their Land possesses, and which are not possessed by Harry's. In Dick's case these superior qualities produce three loaves; in Harry's case, they produce six.

If any one doubts that such is the case, let him imagine our three brothers beginning to quarrel amongst themselves, and Tom and Dick boasting that they were better men than Harry, on the ground that they always brought home more loaves than he. Every one can see what Harry's retort would be, and see also that it is unanswerable. Of course he would say, "I am as good a man as either of you, and my labour produces quite as much as yours. Let us only change fields, and you will see that

The men themselves would be the first to understand this.

soon enough. Let Tom take mine, and let me take his, and I then will bring home fifteen loaves; and he, work as he may, will only bring home nine. It is your b———y land that produces more than mine, not you that produce more than I; and if you deny it, stand out you ———s and I'll fight you." We may also appeal to one of the commonest of our common phrases, in which Harry's supposed contention is every day reiterated. If a farmer is transferred from a bad farm to a good one, and the product of his farming is thereby increased, as it will be, everybody will say, "The good farm *makes* all the difference." This is merely another way of saying, the superior qualities in the soil *produce* all the increase, or—to continue our illustration—the increased number of loaves.

And all the world is not only asserting this truth every day, but is also acting on it; for these extra loaves, produced by the qualities peculiar to superior soils, are neither more nor less than Rent. Rent is the amount of produce which a given amount of exertion obtains from rich land, beyond what it obtains from poor land. Such is the account of rent in which all economists agree; indeed, when once it is understood, the truth of it is self-evident. Mr. Henry George's entire doctrines are built on it; whilst Mill calls it the *pons asinorum* of economics. I have added nothing in the above statement of it to what is stated by all economists, except weight and emphasis to a truth which they do not so much state as imply, and whose importance they seem to have overlooked. This truth is like a note on a piano, which they have all of them sounded lightly amongst other notes. I have sounded it by itself, and have emphasised it with the loud pedal—the truth that rent is for all practical purposes not the product of Land and Human Exertion combined, but the product of Land solely, as separate from Human Exertion and distinct from it.

The above doctrine of Rent is not a landlord's doctrine. It would hold true of a Socialistic State as well as of any other.

And here let me pause for a moment to point out a fact which, though it illustrates the above truth further, I should not mention here if it were not for the following reason. Rent forms the subject of so much social and party prejudice that what I have just been urging may be received by certain readers with suspicion, and regarded as some special pleading on behalf of landlords. I wish therefore to point out clearly that the existence of rent and the payment of rent is not peculiar to our existing system of landlordism. Rent must arise, under any social arrangement, from all soils which are better than the poorest soil cultivated: it must be necessarily paid to somebody; and that somebody must necessarily be the owner. If a peer or a squire is the owner, it is paid to the peer or squire; if the cultivator is the owner, the cultivator pays it to himself; if the land were nationalised and the State were to become the owner, the cultivator would have to pay it away to the State.

In order that the reader may fully realise this, let us go back to our three brothers, of whom the only two who paid rent at all, paid it, according to our supposition, to themselves; and let us imagine that Harry—the brother who pays no rent to anybody, because his field produces none, has a sweetheart who lives close to Tom's field, or who sits and sucks blackberries all day in its hedge; and that Harry is thus anxious to exchange fields with Tom, in order that he may be cheered at

It is easy to see how Rent arises, under any conditions, from all superior soils.

his work by the smiles of the beloved object. Now if Tom were to assent to Harry's wishes without making any conditions, he would be not only humouring the desire of Harry's heart, but he would be making him a present of six loaves daily; and this, we may assume, he certainly would not do; nor would Harry, if he knew anything of human nature, expect or even ask him to do so. If Tom, however, were on good terms with his brother, he might quite conceivably be willing to meet his wishes, could it be but arranged that he should be no loser by doing so; and this could be accomplished in one way only—namely, by arranging that, since Harry would gain six loaves each day by the exchange, and Tom would lose them, Harry should send these six loaves every day to Tom; and thus, whilst Harry was a gainer from a sentimental point of view, the material circumstances of both of them would remain what they were before. Or we may put the arrangement in more familiar terms. The loaves in question we have supposed to be worth fourpence each; so we may assume that instead of actually sending the loaves, Harry sends his brother

OF WHOEVER OWNS THE LAND

two shillings a day, or twelve shillings a week, or thirty pounds a year. Tom's field, as we have said, is twelve acres; therefore, Harry pays him a rent of fifty shillings an acre. And Tom's case is the case of every landlord, no matter whether the landlord is a private person or the State—a peer who lets his land, a peasant like Tom who cultivates it, or a State which allows the individual to occupy but not to own it. Rent represents an advantage which is naturally inherent in certain soils; and whoever owns this advantage—either the State or the private person—must of necessity either take the rent, or else make a present of it to certain favoured individuals.

It should further be pointed out that this doctrine of Rent, though putting so strict a limit on the product that can be assigned to Labour, interferes with no view that the most ardent Socialist or Radical may entertain with regard to the moral rights of the labourer. If any one contends that the men who labour on the land, and who pay away part of the produce as rent to other persons, ought by rights to retain the whole produce for themselves, he is perfectly at liberty to do so, for anything that has been urged here. For the real meaning of such a contention is, not that the labourers do not already keep everything that is produced by their labour, but that they ought to own their land instead of hiring it, and so keep everything that is produced by the land as well.

This doctrine of Rent, then, which I have tried to make absolutely clear, involves no special pleading on behalf either of landlord or tenant, of rich or poor. It can be used with equal effect by Tory, Radical, or Socialist, and it would be as true of a Socialistic State as it is of any other. I have insisted on it here for one reason only. It illustrates, and is the fundamental example of, the following great principle—that in all cases where Human Exertion is applied to Land which yields only enough wealth to maintain the man exerting himself, practical logic compels us to attribute the entire product to his exertion, and to take the assumption that his exertion produces this much as our starting-point. But in all other cases—that is to say in all cases where the same exertion results in an increased product, we attribute the increase—we attribute the added product—not to Human Exertion, which is present equally in both cases, but to some cause which is present in the second case, and was not present in the first: that is to say, to some superior quality in the soil.

And now let us put this in a more general form. When two or more causes produce a given amount of wealth, and when the same causes with some other cause added to them produce a greater amount, the excess of the last amount over the first is produced by the added cause; or conversely, the added cause produces precisely that proportion of the total by which the total would be diminished if the added cause were withdrawn.

It is on this principle that the whole reasoning in the present book is based; and having seen how it enables us to discriminate between the amounts of wealth produced respectively by Human Exertion and Land, let us go on to see how it will enable us likewise to discriminate what is produced by Capital.

CHAPTER III

Of the Products of Machinery or Fixed Capital, as distinguished from the Products of Human Exertion.

<small>To understand how much of the gross product is made by Capital, it will be well to turn from agriculture to manufactures;</small>

LAND, which in economics means everything that the earth produces and the areas it offers for habitation, is of course in a sense at the bottom of every industry. But if we wish to understand the case of Capital, it will be well to turn from agriculture to industry of another kind; the reason being that the part which Capital plays in agriculture is not only, comparatively speaking, small, but is also a part which, when we are first approaching the subject, is comparatively ill fitted for purposes of illustration.

<small>As Capital plays in manufactures a more obvious part.</small>

What is best fitted for the purpose of illustration is Capital applied to manufactures; and it is best at first not to consider all such Capital, but to confine our attention to one particular part of it. I must explain to the reader exactly what I mean.

CAPITAL OF TWO KINDS

People constantly speak of Capital as being a sensitive thing—a movable thing—a thing that is easily driven away—that can be transferred from one place to another by a mere stroke of the pen. We all of us know the phrases. But though they express a truth, it is partial truth only. Capital before it is employed, when it is lying, let us say, in a bank, to the credit of a Company that has not yet begun operations—Capital, under such circumstances, is no doubt altogether movable; for before it is employed it exists as credit only. But the moment it is employed in manufacture, a very considerable part of it is converted into things that are very far from movable—into such things as buildings and heavy machinery; and only a part remains movable—namely that reserved for wages. For example, M'Culloch estimates that the average cost of a factory is about *one hundred pounds* for every operative to be employed in it; whilst the yearly wages of each adult male would now on the average, be about *sixty pounds*. Thus, if a factory is started which will employ *one thousand* men, and if the wages of all of them have to be paid out of

Book II. Ch. III.
Capital, when actually employed, is of two kinds:
Fixed Capital, such as plant and machinery; and Wage Capital.

Capital for a year, the amount reserved for wages will be *sixty thousand pounds*, whilst *a hundred thousand pounds* will have been converted into plant and buildings. Most people are familiar with the names given by economists to distinguish the two forms into which employed capital divides itself. The part which is reserved for, and paid in wages, is called "Circulating Capital"; that which is embodied in buildings and machinery is called "Fixed Capital." Of Circulating Capital—or, as we may call it, Wage Capital—we will speak presently. We will speak at first of Fixed Capital only; and of this we will take the most essential part, namely machinery; and for convenience sake we will omit the accidental part, namely buildings, which render merely the passive service of shelter.

The Capital embodied in machinery is what, for our present purpose, we must first consider.

Now in any operation of manufacturing raw material, or—what means the same thing —conveying raw material, say water or coal or fish, to the places where they are to be consumed, certain machines or appliances are necessary to enable the operation to take place well. Thus fish or coal could hardly be carried without a basket, whilst water could

BY MACHINERY OR FIXED CAPITAL

certainly not be carried without some vessel, nor in many places raised from its source without a rope and pail. For all purposes therefore of practical argument and calculation, appliances of these most simple and indispensable kinds are merged in Human Exertion, just as is the case with the poorest kind of Land, and are not credited separately with any portion of the result. We do not say the man raised so much water, and the rope and the pail so much. We say the man raised the whole. But the moment we have to deal with appliances of an improved kind, by which the result is increased, whilst the labour remains the same, the case of the appliances becomes analogous to that of superior soils; and a portion of the result can be assigned to them, distinct from the result of Labour.

We shall see that machinery adds to the product of Labour in the same way that a superior soil adds to it;

Let us suppose, for instance, that a village gets all its water from a cistern, to keep which replenished takes the labour of ten men, constantly raising the water by means of pails and ropes, and then carrying it to the cistern, up a steep wearisome hill. These men, we will say, receive each *one pound* a week, the village thus paying for its water *five*

As a certain simple instance will show.

hundred pounds a year, the whole of which sum goes in the remuneration of labour. We will suppose, further, that the amount of water thus obtained is *a thousand* gallons daily, each man raising and carrying *a hundred* gallons; and that this supply, though sufficient for the necessities of the villagers, is not sufficient for their comfort. They would gladly have twice that amount; but they are not able to pay for it. Such is the situation with which we start. We have *a thousand* gallons of water supplied daily by the exertion of ten men, or *a hundred* gallons by the exertion of each of them.

And now let us suppose that the village is suddenly presented with a pumping-engine, having a handle or handles at which five of these men can work simultaneously, and by means of which they, working no harder than formerly, can raise twice the amount of water that was formerly raised by ten men— namely *two thousand* gallons daily, instead of *one thousand*. The villagers, therefore, have now *a thousand* gallons daily which they did not have before; and to what is the supply of this extra quantity due? It is not due to Labour. The Labour involved can produce no more than formerly; indeed it must produce less; for its quality is unchanged, and it is halved in quantity. Obviously, then, the extra *thousand* gallons are due to the pumping-engine, and this not in a mere theoretical sense, but in the most practical sense possible; for this extra supply appears in the cistern as soon as the engine is present, and would cease to appear if the engine were taken away.

And here let me pause for a moment, as I did when I was discussing land, to point out a fact which at the present stage of argument has no logical place, but which should be realised by the reader, in order to avoid misconception: namely, the fact that the extra water-supply which is due to the pumping-engine, will necessarily be the property of whoever owns the engine, just as rent will be the property of whoever owns the land that yields it. We supposed just now that the owner of the engine was the village. We supposed that the engine was presented to it. Consequently the village owned the whole extra *thousand* gallons. It had not to pay for them. But let us suppose instead that the

It may be also observed that the added product will go to the owner of the machine, just as rent goes to the owner of the land.

engine was the property of some stranger. Just as necessarily in that case the gallons would belong to him; and he could command payment for them, just as if he had carried them to the cistern himself. We supposed that the village was able to pay *five hundred pounds* for its water; and that it really wanted, for its convenience, twice as much as it could obtain for that sum expended on human labour. The owner of the pumping-engine, by allowing the village to use it, doubles the water-supply, and halves the labour bill. The expenditure on labour sinks from *five hundred pounds* to *two hundred and fifty pounds;* and the owner of the pumping-engine can, it is needless to say, command the *two hundred and fifty pounds* which is saved to the village by its use. In actual life, no doubt, the bargain would be less simple; because in actual life there would be a number of rival pumping-engines, whose owners would reduce, by competition, the price of the extra water; but whatever the price might be, the principle would remain the same. The price or the value of the water would go to the owner of the engine; and it would fail to do so only if one thing happened—if the owner refused to receive it, and, for some reason or other, made the village a free gift of what the village would be perfectly willing to buy. In this truth there is nothing that makes for or against Socialism. The real contention of the Socialist is simply this—not that labour makes what is actually made by machinery; but that labourers ought to own the machinery, and for that reason appropriate what is made by it. A machine or engine, in fact, which is used to assist labour is, in its quality of a producing agent, just as separate from the labour with which it co-operates, as a donkey, in its quality of a carrying agent, is distinct from its master, if the master is walking along carrying one sack of corn, and guiding the donkey who walks carrying seven.

And this brings us back into the line of our main argument; the comparison just made being a very apt and helpful illustration of it. Every machine may be looked on as a kind of domestic animal, and each new machine as an animal of some new species; which animals co-operate with men in the production of certain products: and the point

A machine, then, as a productive agent, is as distinct from human labour as are the efforts of an animal.

I am urging on the reader may accordingly be put thus. When a man, or a number of men, without one of these animals to assist them, produce a certain amount of some particular product, and with the assistance of one of these animals produce a much larger amount, the added quantity is produced not by the men, but by the animal—or, to drop back again into the language of fact, by the machine.

<small>The history of the cotton industry is a remarkable illustration of this.</small> I have taken an imaginary case of drawing and pumping water, because the operation is of an exceedingly simple kind. We will now turn from the imaginary world to the real, and clench what has been said by an illustration from the history of our own country—and from that period which at present we specially have in view—namely the close of the last century.

From the year 1795 to the year 1800, the amount of cotton manufactured in this country was on the average about *thirty-seven million pounds* weight annually: ten years before it was only *ten million pounds*; ten years before that, only *four million pounds*; and during the previous fifty years it had been less than *two and a half million pounds*. The amount manufactured, up to the end of this last-named period, was limited by the fact that spinning was a much slower process than weaving. It was performed by means of an apparatus known as "the one-thread wheel." No other spinning-machine existed; and it was the opinion of experts, about the year 1770, that it would hardly be possible in the course of the next thirty years, by collecting and training to the spinning trade every hand that could be secured for such a purpose, to raise the annual total to so much as *five million pounds*. As a matter of fact, however, *five million pounds* were spun in the year 1776. In six years' time, the original product had been doubled. In ten years, it had been more than quadrupled; in twenty years, it had increased nearly elevenfold; and in five and twenty years, it had increased fifteenfold.[1]

To what, then, was this extraordinary increase due? It was due to the invention and introduction of new spinning machinery

For every pound of cotton spun by labour, Arkwright's machinery spun fourteen pounds.

[1] From 1716 to 1770 the cotton manufactured in this country annually averaged under *two and a half million pounds* weight. From 1771 to 1775 it was *four million seven hundred thousand pounds*. From 1781 to 1785 it was *eleven million pounds*. From 1791 to 1795 it was *twenty-six million pounds;* and from 1795 to 1800 it was *thirty-seven million pounds*.

—especially to the machines invented by Hargraves and Arkwright, and the successive application of horse-power, water-power, and lastly of steam-power, to driving them. Previous to the year 1770, such a thing as a cotton-mill was unknown. During the ten following years, about forty were erected in Great Britain; in the six years following there were erected a hundred more; and from that time forward their number increased rapidly, till they first absorbed, and then more than absorbed, the whole population that had previously conducted the industry in their own homes. As we follow the history of the manufacture into the present century, a large part of the increasing gross produce is to be set down to the increase in the employed population; but during the twenty-five years with which we have just been dealing, the number of hands employed in spinning had not more than doubled,[1] whilst the amount of cotton manufactured had increased by fifteen hundred per cent.

---

[1] Pitt estimated that the hands employed in spinning increased from forty thousand to eighty thousand between the years 1760 and 1790.

THE IRON INDUSTRY OF GREAT BRITAIN 119

It is therefore evident that the increase during this period is due almost entirely, not to human exertion, but to machinery.[1]

And next, with more brevity, let us consider the manufacture of iron. By and by we shall come back to the subject; so it will be enough here to mention a single fact connected with it. From about the year 1740, when a careful and comprehensive inquiry into the matter was made, up to the year 1780, the average produce of each smelting furnace in the country was *two hundred and ninety-four tons* of iron annually. Towards the close of this period machinery had been invented by which a blast was produced of a strength that had been unknown previously; and in the year 1788, the average product of each of these same furnaces

The manufacture of iron offers a similar example.

---

[1] Were any confirmation of this conclusion needed, it is afforded us by the fact that in 1786 a spinner received *ten shillings* a pound for spinning cotton of a certain quality : in 1795 he had received only *eightpence*, or a fifteenth part of ten shillings ; and yet in the course of a similar day's labour, he made more money than he had been able to do under the former scale of payment. The price of spinning No. 100 was *ten shillings* per pound in 1786 ; in 1793, *two shillings and sixpence.* The subsequent drop to *eightpence* coincided with the application of machinery to the working of the mule.

was *five hundred and ninety-five tons*, or very nearly double what it had been previously. An extra *two hundred and fifty tons* was produced from each furnace annually: and if we attribute the whole of the former product to human exertion, *two hundred and fifty tons* at all events was the product of the new machinery; since if that had been destroyed, the product, in proportion to the expenditure of exertion, would at once have sunk back to what it had been forty-eight years earlier.

<small>The products, then, of Capital embodied in machinery are easily distinguishable from the products of Labour.</small>

Here, then, we have before us the two principal manufactures of this country, as they were during the closing years of the last century; and we have seen that in each a definite portion of the product was due to a certain kind of capital, as distinct from human exertion—distinct from human exertion in precisely the same way, as we have already seen land to be, when we find it producing rent; and we have seen further that the products both of this kind of Capital and of Land, are to be distinguished from those of Human Exertion on precisely similar principles.[1]

---

[1] Were this work a treatise on political economy, rather than a work on practical politics, in which only the simplest

Machinery, however,—or fixed capital, of which we have taken machinery as the type,— is only a part of Capital considered as a whole. We have still to deal with the part that is reserved for and spent in wages; and this will introduce us to an entirely new subject —a subject which as yet I have not so much as hinted at—namely human exertion considered in an entirely new light.

BOOK II. CH. III.

In the next chapter we will consider the products of Wage Capital.

and most fundamental economic principles are insisted on, I should have here introduced a chapter on the special and peculiar part which fixed capital, other than machinery, plays in agriculture. I have not done so, however, for fear of interrupting the thread of the main argument; but it will be useful to call the reader's attention to the subject in a note.

It was explained in the last chapter that rent (to speak with strict accuracy) is not to be described as the product of superior soils, but rather as the product of the qualities which make such soils superior—qualities which are present in them and which in poorer soils are absent. Now in speaking of rent, we assumed these superior qualities to be natural. As a matter of fact, however, in highly cultivated countries, many of them are artificial. They have been added to the soil by human exertion—for instance by the process of draining; or they have been actually placed in the soil, as by the process of manuring. In this way land and capital merge and melt into one another, and illustrate each other's functions as productive agents. It is impossible to imagine a more complete and beautiful example of the relation between the two. At this point the rent of Capital and the rent of Land become indistinguishable.

CHAPTER IV

Of the Products of Circulating Capital, or Wage Capital, as distinguished from the Products of Human Exertion.

<small>Wage Capital enables men to undertake work which will not support them till a considerable time has elapsed.</small>

CIRCULATING Capital, or, as it is better to call it, Wage Capital, is practically a store of those things which wages are used to buy—that is to say the common necessaries of subsistence. And the primary function—the simplest and most obvious function—which such Capital performs is this: it enables men, by supplying them with the means of living, to undertake long operations, which when completed will produce much or be of much use, but which until they are completed will produce nothing and be of no use, and will consequently supply nothing themselves to the men whilst actually engaged in them.

Let us imagine, for instance, a tunnel which

pierces a range of mountains, and facilitates communication between two populous cities. Five hundred navvies, we will say, have to work five years to make it. Now if two yards of tunnel were made every day, and if each yard could be used as soon as made, the tolls of passengers would at once yield a daily revenue which would provide the navvies with subsistence, as their work proceeded. But as a matter of fact until the last day's work is done, and the end of the fifth year sees the piercing of the mountain completed, the tunnel is as useless as it was when it was only just begun, and when it was nothing more than a shallow cavity in a rock. Five years must elapse before a single toll is paid, and before the tunnel itself supplies a single human being with the means of providing bread for even a single day. The possibility then of the tunnel being made at all, depends on the existence of a five-years' supply of necessaries, for which indirectly the tunnel will pay hereafter, but in producing or providing which, it has had no share whatever.

A tunnel is a good instance of such work.

Wage Capital, in fact, imparts to industry the power of waiting for its own results. This is its simplest, its most obvious, and its primeval function. It has been the function of such capital from the days of the earliest civilisations; and it is, indeed, its fundamental function still: but in the modern world it is far from being its principal function. I call its principal functions in the modern world the functions by which during the past century and a quarter it has produced results so incomparably, and so increasingly greater, than were ever produced by it in the whole course of preceding ages.

What this function is must be explained very clearly and carefully. It is not to enable labourers to wait for the results of their labours. It is to enable the exceptional knowledge, ingenuity, enterprise, and productive genius of a few men so to animate, to organise, and direct the average physical exertions of the many, as to improve, to multiply, or to hasten the results of that exertion without increasing its quantity. All civilisations, ancient as well as modern, have involved, in a certain sense, the direction by the few of the many. The temples and palaces of early Egypt and Assyria, which excite the wonder of modern engineers and architects by the size of the blocks of stone used in their astounding structure, are monuments of a control, absolute and unlimited and masterly, exercised by a few human minds over millions of human bodies. But in that control, as exercised in the ancient world, one element was wanting which is the essence of modern industry. When the masters of ancient labour wished to multiply commodities, or to secure an increase of power for accomplishing some single work, the sole means known to them was to increase the number of labourers; and when one thousand slaves were insufficient, to reinforce them with (let us say) four thousand more. The masters of modern labour pursue a new and essentially opposite course. Instead of seeking in such a case to secure four thousand new labourers, they seek to endow one thousand with the industrial power of five. If Nebuchadnezzar had set himself to tunnel a mountain, he could have hastened the work only by flogging more slaves to it. The modern contractor, in co-operation with the modern inventor, instead of flogging labour, would assist it with tram-lines, trucks, and

The modern employer in this respect differs from the ancient.

boring engines. In other words, whereas in former ages the aim of the employing class was simply to secure the service of an increasing quantity of labour, the aim of the employing class in the present age is to increase the productive power of the same quantity. The employing class in former ages merely forced the employed to exert their own industrial faculties, and appropriated what those faculties produced. The employing class of the present age not only commands the employed, but it co-operates with them by lending them faculties which they do not themselves possess. It applies to the guidance of the muscles of the most ordinary worker the profoundest knowledge of science, all the strength of will, all the spirit of enterprise, and the exceptional aptitude for affairs, that distinguish the most gifted and the vigorous characters of the day. And it is the peculiar modern function of Capital, as spent in Wages, to enable this result to take place.

Wage Capital in the modern world is the means by which exceptional intellect is lent to Labour.

Let us consider how it does so. Socialists tell us that Capitalism in the modern world means merely the appropriation by the few of all the materials of production, so that the many

Wage Capital does this in a way which the socialistic definition of

must either work as the few bid them, or must starve. But this is a very small part of what modern Capitalism means, and it is not the essential part, nor does it even suggest the essential part. The majority of men must always work or starve. Nature, not modern Capitalism, is responsible for that necessity. The essential difference which modern Capitalism has introduced into the situation is this—and it is an enormous difference—that whereas in former ages the livelihood of a man was contingent on his working in the best way that the average man knew, modern Capitalism has made his livelihood contingent on his working in the best way that exceptional men know. Now this best way, as we shall see more clearly presently, does not involve the forcing of each man to work harder, or the exacting from him any more difficult effort. It involves merely the supplying him with a constant external guide for even his minutest actions— a guide for every movement of arm and hand, or a pattern of each of the objects which are the direct result of these movements; and consequently the one thing which before all others it requires is constant obedience or

Capital altogether ignores.

conformity to such guides and patterns. The entire industrial progress of the modern world has depended, and depends altogether on this constant obedience being secured; and the possession of Wage Capital by the employing class is the sole means which is possible in the modern world of securing it. In the ancient world the case would no doubt have been different. The lash of the taskmaster, the fear of prison, of death, of torture, were then available for the stimulation and organisation of Labour. But they are available no longer. The masses of civilised humanity have taken this great step—they have risen from the level on which they could be driven to industrial obedience, to the level on which they must be induced to it. Obedience of some sort is a social necessity now as ever, and always must be: but social necessity spoke merely to the fear of the slave; it speaks to the will and the reason of the free labourer. The free labourer may be, and must be, in one or other of two positions. He may work for himself, consuming or selling his own produce; or he may work for an employer, who pays him wages, and exacts in return for them not work only, but work performed in a certain prescribed way. The first position is that of the peasant proprietor or the hand-loom weaver. The second is that of the employee in a mill or factory. In both cases, the voice of social necessity, or of society, speaks to the man's reason, informing him of the homely fact that he cannot live unless he labours: but in the first case, the voice of society cries to him out of the ground, "You will get no food unless you labour in some way"; and in the second case it cries to him from the mouths of the wisest and strongest men, "You will get no food unless you consent to labour in the best way."[1]

In other words, Wage Capital in the modern world promotes that growth of wealth by which the modern world is distinguished, simply because Wage Capital is the vehicle by which the exceptional qualities of the few communicate themselves to the whole industrial community. The real principle of progress and production is not in the Capital, but in the

Wage Capital is merely the means by which intellect impresses itself as Labour;

---

[1] In a state where the employing class were physically the masters of the employed, Wage Capital would be unnecessary for the employer. A system of forced labour might take its place.

qualities of the men who control it; just as the vital force which goes to make a great picture is not in the brush, but in the great painter's hand; or as the skill which pilots a coach and four through London is not in the reins, but in the hand of the expert coachman.

<small>BOOK II. CH. IV.</small>

<small>As we can see by following the steps by which a company would introduce some new machine.</small>

This can easily be seen by turning our attention once again to machinery, and supposing that a company is floated for the improved manufacture of something by means of some new invention. The directors must of course begin with securing a site for the factory; but with this exception their entire initial expenditure will directly or indirectly consist in the payment of wages—in purchasing the services of a certain number of men by whose exertions certain masses of raw material are to be produced and fashioned into certain definite forms—that is to say, into the new machinery and a suitable building to protect it.

<small>The whole success of such a company depends on the amount of intellect used in the</small>

Now, the powers of these men resemble a mass of fluid metal which is capable of being run into any variety of mould. If the directors were bound by no articles of association, and if, at their first board meeting, before they had entered into any contract for the machinery, some other invention for the manufacture of some other commodity were suddenly brought to their notice, and happened to take their fancy, the men they were on the point of employing to produce one kind of machinery might, with equal ease, be employed to produce another. We will assume that the machinery which the men are set to produce actually is a great improvement on anything of the kind used hitherto, and ends in adding greatly to the productive powers of the nation; but, so far as the men are concerned whose exertions are paid for out of the capital of the company, the machinery might just as well have been absolutely valueless—a mere aggregation of wheels and axles, as meaningless as a madman's dream. What makes their exertions not only useful instead of useless, but more useful than any exertion similarly applied had ever been hitherto, is, firstly, the ingenuity of the inventor of the new machine; secondly, the judgment of the promoters and directors of the company; and lastly, the confidence in their judgment felt by the subscribing public. Or, we may suppose the inventor to have himself supplied the Capital, and to unite in himself the parts of the directors and the shareholders. In that case the exertions of the men employed derive their value entirely from the talent of this one man. The men employed by him, we will say, number a thousand, and the Wage Capital he owns and administers aids and increases production only because it is the means by which the one man induces the thousand to accept him as the steersman of their exertions, and to allow him to direct their course towards new and remote results which for them lie hidden behind the horizon of contemporary habit or ignorance.

The case of Arkwright's spinning-frame illustrates this.

Let us take an actual case—the case of Arkwright's spinning-frame. This invention, which was destined to influence the prosperity of so many millions, was in great danger of being altogether lost, simply on account of the difficulty experienced by the inventor in securing sufficient capital to construct and perfect his machine, and, what was equally necessary, to exhibit it in actual use. After many rebuffs and disappointments, a sum was at last

advanced him by a certain firm of bankers—
the Messrs. Wright of Nottingham; but before
the preliminary experiments had advanced far
their courage failed them, they repented of
what they had done, and they passed the
inventor on to two other capitalists whose
insight was fortunately keener, and whose
characters were more courageous. These
gentlemen, Mr. Need and Mr. Strutt of Derby,
took Arkwright into partnership, and by means
of the Capital which they placed at his disposal,
his machine, which till now had existed only in
his own brain and in a few unfinished models,
was before long in operation, and a new industrial era was inaugurated. Now, to the accomplishment of this result Wage Capital was
essential; but it was essential only as the
means of giving effect to the genius and strong
character of certain specially gifted persons—
Arkwright with his marvellous inventive
genius, Messrs. Need and Strutt with their
sagacity and spirit and enterprise. If it had
not been for the qualities of these three men,
the wages paid to the labourers who made the
machine of Arkwright would have probably
been paid indeed to the very same labourers,

BOOK II.
CH. IV.

but their exertions would have been directed to producing some different product — some product which added nothing to the existing powers of the community.

Now machinery is necessarily Wage Capital congealed;

Machinery, therefore, or Fixed Capital, though it differs as soon as it is made from Capital employed in wages, is the result of the use of such Capital, and is indeed but another form of it. And now comes the point on which I am concerned to insist here: that conversely Wage Capital, when employed so as to increase the productivity of labour,—in other words when employed by men with the requisite capacity,—is in its essence but another form of machinery. Machinery may be called congealed Wage Capital. Wage Capital may be called fluid machinery. For the function of both — namely, to increase wealth — is the same, and they fulfil this function by means of the same virtue residing in them. It is easy to see the truth of this. The increase of wealth means the improvement and multiplication of commodities which reward the exertions of the same number of men. The number and quality of these commodities are increased by application of Capital, because Capital enables persons

POTENTIAL MACHINERY 135

who are exceptionally gifted to control and direct the exertions of the majority; and Capital, as embodied in machinery, differs from Capital continuously employed in wages, only because the former gives us machinery which is inanimate, and the latter, machinery which is living. For a thousand men so organised as to produce some given product or result, and to produce it with the greatest precision or in the least possible time, are to all intents and purposes as much an invention and a machine as a thousand wheels or rollers adjusted for a similar purpose.

{BOOK II. CH. IV.}

All Capital, therefore, in all its distinctively modern applications—all those applications which have caused what is called industrial progress—is virtually this, and this only: it represents is the exceptional capacities of one set of men applied to the average capacities of another set. We may accordingly include all Capital —fixed and circulating—under one head, and say of it as a whole what in the last chapter was said of machinery: that when by its application to the exertions of a given number of men a larger product results than resulted from them before it was applied, Capital is to

{And therefore all Capital, equally with Wage Capital, represents the control of Intellect over Labour— or one kind of Human Exertion over another.}

be credited with producing the amount of the increase; or—to put the same thing in another way—with the amount of the decrease which would result if its application were withdrawn.

How this is the case with machinery I have already illustrated by examples. It is less easy to illustrate by examples, but equally easy to see how it is the case with Capital continuously employed as wages. It is less easy to select illustrations, because the whole of modern progress is itself one great, though infinitely complex example of it; and it will be enough here as we shall recur to the subject presently, to consider one obvious and very familiar fact. Many new commodities, and many new methods of production, depend on the invention not of new machines, but of new processes. The Capital employed in working a new process is mainly employed as wages, by the administration of which the actions of the workmen are guided, controlled, and organised. Thus if fifty men, working independently and selling their own produce, produce a hundred articles of a certain sort weekly, and another fifty men, working for a wage-paying employer, produce, owing to the way in which their labour is guided and organised, just double the number of such articles in the same time, we shall say that the hundred extra articles are the product of Wage Capital, just as we should say, if the increased production had been due to the introduction of a machine, that these extra hundred articles were the product of Fixed Capital. And in both cases we should mean, as I am now going to insist more particularly, that they were really the product of the capacities which each kind of Capital represents. This brings us to the heart of the whole problem.

This aspect of the question will be considered further in the next chapter.

CHAPTER V

That the Chief Productive Agent in the modern world is not Labour, but Ability, or the Faculty which directs Labour.

<small>What was said in the last chapter shows that productive Human Exertion is of two kinds, and does not consist only of what is meant by Labour,</small>

I SAID in the last chapter that machinery or Fixed Capital was congealed Wage Capital. But as Wage Capital is metamorphosed into machinery only owing to the fact that it is at once the instrument and the guide of Human Exertion, machinery may be called congealed exertion also. This description of it is but half original; for Socialistic writers have for a long time called it "congealed Labour." But between the two phrases there is a great and fundamental difference, and I now bring them thus together to show what the difference is. The first includes the whole meaning of the second, whereas the second includes only a part of the meaning of the first. Let us take the finest bronze statue that was ever made, and also the worst, the feeblest, the most ridiculous. Both can with equal accuracy be called congealed Labour; but to call them this is just as useless a truism as to call them congealed bronze. It describes the point in which the two statues resemble each other; it tells us nothing of what is far more important—the points in which the two statues differ. They differ because, whilst both are congealed Labour, the one is also congealed imagination of the highest order, the other is also congealed imagination of the lowest. The excellence of the metal and of the casting may be the same in both cases. Or again, let us take a vessel like the *City of Paris*, and let us take also the vessel that was known as the *Bessemer Steamer*. The *Bessemer Steamer* was fitted with a sort of rocking saloon; which, when the vessel rolled, was expected to remain level. The contrivance was a complete failure. The hundreds of thousands of pounds spent on it were practically thrown away, and the structure ended by being sold as old iron. Now these two vessels were equally congealed Labour, and congealed Labour of precisely the same quality; for the workmen employed on the *Bessemer Steamer* were as skilful as those

BOOK II.
CH. V.

As familiar instances will show us.

employed on the *City of Paris*. And yet the Labour in the one case was congealed into a piece of lumber, and in the other case it was congealed into one of the most perfect of those living links by which the lives of two worlds are united. To call both the vessels, then, congealed Labour, only tells us how success resembles failure, not how it differs from it. The *City of Paris* differs from the *Bessemer Steamer* because the *City of Paris* was congealed judgment, and the *Bessemer Steamer* was congealed misjudgment.

It is therefore evident that in *using* Capital so as to make Labour more efficacious, as distinct from *wasting* Capital so as to make Labour nugatory, some other human faculties are involved distinct from the faculty of Labour; and I have employed, except when it would have been mere pedantry to do so, the term "Human Exertion" instead of the term "Labour," because the former includes those other faculties, and the latter does not; or, if it includes them, it entirely fails to distinguish them, and merely confounds them with faculties from which they fundamentally differ. Thus, when I pointed out in the last chapter that

Capital, in so far as it increased the productivity of Labour, was mental and moral energy as applied to muscular energy, I might have said with equal propriety, had my argument advanced far enough, that it was one kind of Human Exertion guiding and controlling another kind. Here we come to the great central fact which forms the key to the whole economic problem : the fact that in the production of wealth two kinds of Human Exertion are involved, and not, as economists have hitherto told us, one—two kinds of exertion absolutely distinct, and, as we shall see presently, following different laws.

Economic writers, like the world in general, do indeed recognise, in an unscientific way, that productive exertion exhibits itself under many various forms ; but their admissions and statements with regard to this point are entirely confused and stultified by the almost ludicrous persistence with which they classify all these forms under the single heading of Labour. Mill, for instance, says that a large part of profits are really wages of the labour of superintendence. He speaks of "the labour of the invention of industrial processes," "the labour

Economic writers vaguely recognise this fact, but have never formally expressed it, or made it a part of their systems.

BOOK II.
CH. V.

They confuse all productive exertion together under the heading of Labour.

of Watt in contriving the steam-engine," and even of "the labour of the savant and the speculative thinker." He employs the same word to describe the effort that invented Arkwright's spinning-frame, and the commonest muscular movement of any one of the mechanics who assisted with hammer or screwdriver to construct it under Arkwright's direction. He employs the same word to describe the power that perfected the electric telegraph, and the power that hangs the wires from pole to pole, like clothes-lines. He confuses under one heading the functions of the employer and the employed—of the men who lead in industry, and of the men who follow. He calls them all labourers, and he calls their work Labour.

Now were the question merely one of literary or philosophical propriety, this inclusive use of the word Labour might be defensible; but we have nothing to do here with the niceties of such trivial criticism. We are concerned not with what a word might be made to mean, but what it practically does mean; and if we appeal to the ordinary use of language, —not only its use by the mass of ordinary men, but its most frequent use by economic writers also,—we shall find that the word Labour has a meaning which is practically settled; and we shall find that this meaning is not an inclusive one, but exclusive. We shall find that Labour practically means muscular Labour, or at all events some form of exertion of which men—common men—are as universally capable, and that it not only never naturally includes any other idea, but distinctly and emphatically excludes it. For instance, when Mill in his *Principles of Political Economy* devotes one of his chapters to the future of the "Labouring Classes," he instinctively uses the phrase as meaning manual labourers. When, as not unfrequently happens, some opulent politician says to a popular audience, "I, too, am a labouring man," he is either understood to be saying something which is only true metaphorically, or is jeered at as saying something which is not true at all. Probably no two men in the United Kingdom have worked harder or for longer hours than Mr. Gladstone and Lord Salisbury; yet no one could call Mr. Gladstone a labour member, or say that Lord Salisbury was an instance of a labouring man being a peer. The Watts, the Stevensons, the

But practically, Labour means muscular or manual exertion.

Whitworths, the Bessemers, the Armstrongs, the Brasseys, are, according to the formal definition of the economists, one and all of them labourers. But what man is there who, if, in speaking of a strike, he were to say that he supported or opposed the claims of Labour, would be understood as meaning the claims of employers and millionaires like these? It is evident that no one would understand him in such a sense; and if he used the word *Labour* thus, he would be merely trifling with language. The word, for all practical purposes, has its meaning unequivocally fixed. It does not mean all Human Exertion; it emphatically means a part of it only. It means muscular and manual exertion, or exertion of which the ordinary man is capable, as distinct from industrial exertion of any other kind; and not only as distinct from it, but as actively opposed to and struggling with it. Since, then, we have to deal with distinct and opposing things, it is idle to attempt to discuss them under one and the same name. To do so would be like describing the Franco-Prussian War with only one name for both armies—the soldiers; or like attempting to explain the composition of

Mental and moral exertion, as applied to production, must therefore be

water, with only one name for oxygen and hydrogen—the gas. Accordingly, for the industrial exertion—exertion moral and mental —which is distinct from Labour and opposed to it, we must find some separate and some distinctive name; and the name which I propose to use for this purpose is Ability.

BOOK II. CH. V. — given another name :

Human Exertion then, as applied to the production of wealth, is of two distinct kinds: Ability and Labour—the former being essentially moral or mental exertion, and only incidentally muscular; the latter being mainly muscular, and only moral or mental in a comparatively unimportant sense. This difference between them, however, though accidentally it is always present, and is what at first strikes the observation, is not the fundamental difference. The fundamental difference is of quite another kind. It lies in the following fact: That Labour is a kind of exertion on the part of the individual, which begins and ends with each separate task it is employed upon, whilst Ability is a kind of exertion on the part of the individual which is capable of affecting simultaneously the labour of an indefinite number of individuals, and thus hastening or perfecting the

In this book it will be called Ability.

There is, however, a deeper distinction between the two than the fact of one being mental and the other muscular.

BOOK II. CH. V.

The vital distinction is that the Labour of one man affects one task only; the Ability of one man may affect an indefinite number.

accomplishment of an indefinite number of tasks.

This vital distinction, hitherto so entirely neglected, should be written in letters of fire on the mind of everybody who wishes to understand, to improve, or even to discuss intelligibly, the economic conditions of a country such as ours. Unless it is recognised, and terms are found to express it, it is impossible to think clearly about the question; much more is it impossible to argue clearly about it: for men's thoughts, even if for moments they are correct and clear, will be presently tripped up and entangled in the language they are obliged to use. Thus, we constantly find that when men have declared all wealth to be due to Labour, more or less consciously including Ability in the term, they go on to speak of Labour and the labouring classes, more or less consciously excluding it; and we can hardly open a review or a newspaper, or listen to a speech on any economic problem, without finding the labouring classes spoken of as "the producers," to the obvious and intentional exclusion of the classes who exercise Ability; whereas it can be demonstrated, as we shall see in another chapter, that of the wealth enjoyed by this country to-day, Labour produces little more than a third.

Let us go back then to the definitions I have just now given, and insist on them and enlarge them and explain them, so as to make them absolutely clear.

Labour, I said, is a kind of exertion on the part of the individual, which begins and ends with each separate task it is employed upon; whilst Ability is a kind of exertion on the part of the individual which is capable of affecting simultaneously the labour of an indefinite number of individuals. Here are some examples. An English navvy, it is said, will do more work in a day than a French navvy; he will dig or wheel away more barrow-loads of earth; but the greater power of the one, if the two work together, has no tendency to communicate itself to the other. The one, let us say, will wheel twelve barrow-loads, whilst the other will wheel ten. We will imagine, then, a gang of ten French navvies, who in a given time wheel a hundred barrow-loads. One of them dies, and his place is

Familiar examples will show the truth of this.

taken by an Englishman. The Englishman wheels twelve loads instead of ten; but the rest of the gang continue to wheel ten only. Let us suppose, however, that the Englishman, instead of being a navvy, is a little cripple who has this kind of ability—that he can show the navvies how to attack with their picks each separate ton of earth in the most efficacious way, and how to run their barrows along the easiest tracks or gradients. He might quite conceivably enable the nine Frenchmen to wheel fifteen barrow-loads in the time that they formerly consumed in wheeling ten; and thus, though the gang contained one labourer less than formerly, yet owing to the presence of one man of ability, the efficacy of its exertions would be increased by fifty per cent. Or again, let us take the case of some machine, whose efficiency is in proportion to the niceness with which certain of its parts are finished. The skilled workman whose labour finishes such parts contributes by doing so to the efficiency of that one machine only; he does nothing to influence the labour of any other workman, or facilitate the production of any other machine similar to it. But the man who, by his inventive ability, makes the machine simpler, or introduces into it some new principle, so that, without requiring so much or such skilled labour to construct it, it will, when constructed, be twice as efficient as before, may, by his ability, affect individual machines without number, and increase the efficiency of the labour of many millions of workmen. Such a case as this is specially worth considering, because it exposes an error to which I shall again refer hereafter—the error often made by economic writers, of treating Ability as a species of Skilled Labour. For Skilled Labour is itself so far from being the same thing as Ability, that it is in some respects more distinct from it than Labour of more common kinds; for the secret of it is less capable of being communicated to other labourers. For instance, one of the most perfect chronometers ever made—namely, that invented by Mudge in the last century—required for its construction Labour of such unusual nicety, that though two specimens, made under the direct supervision of the inventor, went with an accuracy that has

BOOK II.
CH. V.

not since been surpassed, the difficulty of reproducing them rendered the invention valueless. But the great example of this particular truth is to be found in a certain fact connected with the history of the steam-engine—a fact which is little known, whose significance has never been realised, and which I shall mention a little later on. It may thus be said with regard to the production of wealth generally, that it will be limited in proportion to the exceptionally skilled labour it requires, whilst it will be increased in proportion to the exceptional ability that is applied to it.

We shall now be able to describe Capital accurately as *Ability* controlling *Labour*.

The difference, then, between Ability and Labour must be now abundantly clear. As a general rule, there is the broad difference on the surface, that the one is mainly mental and the other mainly muscular; but to this rule there are many exceptions, and the difference in question is accidental and superficial. The essential, the fundamental difference from a practical point of view is, that whilst Labour is the exertion of a single man applied to a single task, Ability is the exertion of a single man applied to an indefinite number of tasks, and an indefinite number of individuals.

And now let us go back to the subject of Capital. I have said that Capital is one kind of Human Exertion guiding and controlling another kind. We can at last express this with more brevity, and say that Capital is Ability guiding and controlling Labour. This is no mere rhetorical or metaphorical statement. It is the accurate expression of what is at once a theoretical truth and an historical fact; and to show the reader that it is so, let me remove certain objections which may very possibly suggest themselves. In the first place, it may be said that Capital belongs constantly to idle and foolish persons, or even indeed to idiots, to all of whom it yields a revenue. This is true; but such an objection altogether ignores the fact that though such persons own the Capital, they do not administer it. An idiot inherits shares in a great commercial house; but the men who manage the business are not idiots. They only pay the idiot a certain sum for allowing his Capital to be made use of by their Ability. It may, however, be said further that many

It is, of course, understood that this definition applies only to Capital used so as actually to make Labour more productive, not to Capital wasted.

men, neither idle nor idiotic, had administered Capital themselves, and had succeeded merely in wasting it. This again is true; but where Capital is wasted the productive powers of the nation are not increased by it. It is, however, a broad historical fact that, by the application of Capital the productive powers of the nation have been increasing continually for more than a hundred years, and are increasing still; and this is the fact, or the phenomenon, which we are engaged in studying. Capital for us, then, means Capital applied successfully; and when I say that Capital is Ability guiding and controlling Labour, it is of Capital applied successfully, and not of Capital wasted, that I must in every case be understood to be speaking; just as if it were said that a battle was won by British bayonets, the bayonets meant would be those that the combatants used, not those that deserters happened to throw away. The fact, indeed, that in certain hands so much Capital is thrown away and wasted, is nothing but a proof of what I say, that as a productive agent Capital represents, and practically *is*, Ability.

It may, however, be said—and the objection is worth noticing—that Capital is a material thing, and Ability a mental thing; and it may be asked how, except metaphorically, the one can be said to be the other? An answer may be given by the analogy of the mind and brain. So long as the mind inhabits and directs a human body, mind and matter are two sides of the same thing. It is only through the brain that mind has power over the muscles; and the brain is powerful only because it is the organ of the mind. Now Ability is to Capital what mind is to the brain; and, like mind and brain, the two terms may be used interchangeably. Capital is that through which the Ability of one set of men acts on the muscles—that is to say, the Labour—of another set, whether by setting Labour to produce machinery, or by so organising various multitudes of labourers that each multitude becomes a single machine in itself, or by settling or devising the uses to which these machines shall be put.

And it will be well, in case any Socialist should happen to read these pages, to point out that my insisting on this fact is no

Capital is to Ability something like what the brain is to the mind.

piece of special pleading on behalf of the private capitalist. The whole of the above argument would apply to Capital, no matter who owned it: individuals, or the community as a whole. For no matter who owned it, or who divided the proceeds of it, the entire control of it would have to be in the hands of Ability. In what, or how many, individuals Ability may be held to reside; how such individuals are best found, tested, and brought forward; and how their power over Capital may be best attained by them—whether as owners, or as borrowers, or as State officials,—is a totally different question, and is in this place beside the point.

And this would be as true of Capital in a Socialistic State as in any other.

At present, it will be enough to sum up what we have seen thus far. The causes of wealth are not, as is commonly said, three: Land, Labour, and Capital. This analysis omits the most important cause altogether, and makes it impossible to explain, or even reason about, the phenomenon of industrial progress. The causes of wealth are four—Land, Labour, Capital, and Ability: the two first being the indispensable elements in the production of any wealth whatsoever; the fourth being the cause of all progress in production; and the third, as it now exists, being the creation of the fourth, and the means through which it operates. These two last, as we shall see presently, may, except for special purposes, be treated as only one, and will be best included under the one term Ability.

And now let us turn back to the condition of this country at the close of the last century, and the reader will see why, at the outset of the above inquiry, I fixed his attention on that particular period.

CHAPTER VI

Of the Addition made during the last Hundred Years by Ability to the Product of the National Labour. This Increment the Product of Ability.

<small>Let us now turn to the history of production in this country during the past hundred years;</small> I HAVE already said something—but in very general terms—of what, at the close of the last century, the wealth of this country was. Let us now consider the subject a little more in detail, though we need not trouble ourselves with a great many facts and figures. The comparatively backward state of Ireland makes it easier to deal with Great Britain only; and the income of Great Britain was then, as I have said already, about *a hundred and forty million pounds* annually. This amount was, as has been said already, also produced by Land, Capital, and Human Exertion, or, as we are now able to put it, by Land, Labour, Capital, and Ability;

and according to the principles which I have already carefully explained, had the statistics of industry been recorded as fully as they are now, we should be able to assign to each cause a definite proportion of the product. Of what the Land produced, as distinct from the three other causes, we are indeed able to speak with sufficient accuracy as it is. It was practically the amount taken in rent; and the amount taken in rent was about *twenty-five million pounds*, or something between a fifth and sixth of the total. But the proportion produced respectively by Labour, Capital, and Ability cannot be determined with the same ease or exactness. There are, however, connected with this question, a number of well-known and highly significant facts, to a few of which I will call the reader's attention.

Between the years 1750 and 1800, the population of Great Britain increased by barely so much as twenty-five per cent. It rose from about eight millions to about ten. Now during that period the number of hands employed in manufactures increased proportionally far faster than the total population. The cotton-spinners, for instance, increased from *forty* to

158   GROWTH OF AGRICULTURAL PRODUCTS

BOOK II.
CH. VI.

eighty thousand.[1] Such being the case, it is of course evident that the increase of agricultural labourers cannot have been very great. It can hardly have been, at the utmost, so much as eighteen per cent.[2] And now let us glance at the history of agricultural products, as indicated by a few typical facts. In the year 1688, the number of sheep in Great Britain was estimated at *twelve millions*. In the year 1774, the number was estimated at almost the same figure; but between the years 1774 and 1800, this *twelve millions* had risen to *twenty millions*. During the same twenty-six years, the number of cattle had increased in almost the same proportion. That is to say, live-stock had increased by seventy-five per cent. Between the years 1750 and 1780 there was an average annual increase in agricultural capital of *seven million three hundred thousand pounds*. But from the years 1780 and 1800 there was an average annual increase of *twenty-six million pounds;* whilst between the years

[1] This was Pitt's computation. *See* Lecky, *History of England during the Eighteenth Century*, vol. vi. chap. xxiii.

[2] The amount of land, formerly waste, that was added to the cultivable area during the last century, was in England and Wales not more than sixteen per cent of the total.

GROWTH OF PRODUCTION OF IRON 159

1750 and 1800 the farmer's income had very nearly doubled,[1] and the total products of agriculture had increased sixty per cent.

And now let us turn to manufactures. These, as a whole, had advanced more slowly; but the advance of certain of them had been yet more rapid and striking. It will be enough to mention two: the manufacture of cotton, to which I have called attention already; and an industry yet more important— the manufacture of iron. The amount of pig-iron produced annually in Great Britain during the earlier part of the last century was not more than *twenty thousand tons*;[2] at the close of the century it was more than *a hundred and eighty thousand*. What may have been the increase in the amount of labour employed, cannot be said with certainty; but it cannot have been comparable to the increase of the product, which was, as we have just seen, eight hundred per cent;

BOOK II.
CH. VI.

And in manufactures,

That had recently taken place at the close of the last century.

---

[1] The rental of Great Britain in 1750 was about *thirteen million five hundred thousand pounds*, and in 1800 about *twenty-nine million six hundred thousand pounds*. According to the estimates of Arthur Young, the farmer's income somewhat more. The wages of Agricultural Labour had not risen proportionately.

[2] See *Encyclopædia Britannica*, first and earlier editions.

and it may be mentioned that one single set of inventions, in the course of eight years, nearly doubled the product of each individual smelting furnace.[1] As to the cotton industry, our information is more complete. The amount of labour was doubled in forty years. The product was increased fifteen-fold in twenty-five.

My present aim, however, is to make no exact calculation respecting the extent to which production, taken as a whole, had during the period in question outstripped the increase of Labour; but merely to show the reader that the extent was very large; and that, according to the principles explained already, it was due altogether to the operation of Capital and Ability—or, to speak more exactly, of Ability operating through Capital. The truth of this statement with regard to the increase of manufactures has been shown and illustrated by the instance of Arkwright and the cotton industry. It will be well to mention at this point several analogous instances taken from

---

[1] See *Encyclopædia Britannica*, first and earlier editions. The product of each smelting furnace in use in 1780 was *two hundred and ninety-four tons* annually. In 1788, these same furnaces were producing, by the aid of new inventions, *five hundred and ninety-four tons*.

the history of agriculture. Elkington, who inaugurated a new system of drainage, will supply us with one. One still more remarkable is supplied by Bakewell, who may be said to have played in practical life a part resembling that which Darwin has played in speculation. He discovered the method of improving the breeds of sheep and cattle by a system of selection and crossing that was not before known; and it was owing to the ability of this one man that "the breed of animals in England," as Mr. Lecky points out, "was probably more improved in the course of a single fifty years than in all the recorded centuries that preceded it." The close connection of such improvements with Capital is the constant theme of Arthur Young, though he was not consciously anything of a political economist, nor did he attempt to express his opinion in scientific language. But a still more effective witness is a distinguished modern Radical, Professor Thorold Rogers, who, though always ready, and, as many people would say, eager to espouse the side of Labour as against Capital and Ability,—especially when the two last belonged to the landed class

BOOK II. CH. VI.

And that Labour cannot really have produced the whole.

—is yet compelled to assert as emphatically as Young himself, that the Ability and the Capital of this very class were in the last century "the pioneers of agricultural progress"—a progress which he illustrates by these picturesque examples: that it raised the average weight of the fatted ox from 400 lbs. to 1200 lbs., and increased the weight of the average fleece fourfold.

Therefore it is plain that Labour would not have created the whole of the national income a hundred years ago. But for argument's sake we will concede that it produced the whole.

It will therefore be apparent to every reader, that of the income of Great Britain at the close of the last century, Ability and Capital, as distinct from Labour, created a considerable part, though we need not determine what part. Accordingly, since the income of Great Britain, with a population of *ten millions,* was at that time about *a hundred and forty million pounds,* or *fourteen pounds* per head,[1] it is evident that the Labour of a

[1] According to Arthur Young's estimates, the earnings of an agricultural family, consisting of seven persons all capable of work, would be about *fifty-one pounds* annually. This gives a little over *seven pounds* a head; but when the children and others not capable of work are taken into account the average is considerably lower. The wages, however, of the artisan class being higher, the average amount per head taken by the whole working population would be about *seven pounds.*

population of *ten millions* was quite incapable, a hundred years ago, of producing by itself as much as *fourteen pounds* per head.¹ I will, however, merely for the sake of argument, and of keeping a calculation I am about to make far within the limits which strict truth would warrant, make a preposterous concession to any possible objector. I will concede that Labour by itself produced the entire value in question, and that Ability, as distinct from Labour, had nothing at all to do with it. I will concede that the faculties which produced the machines of Arkwright, which had already turned steam into an infant Hercules of industry, and was pouring into this island the wealth of the farthest Indies, were faculties of the same order as those which were possessed by any waggoner who had driven the same waggon along the same ruts for a lifetime. And I will now proceed to the calculation I spoke of. I shall state it first, and establish its truth afterwards.

It will be seen, from what has just been The whole income of

¹ About £1 : 12s. per head would have to be set down to land, were the land question being dealt with. But for the purpose of the above discussion, land may be ignored, as it does not affect the problem.

BOOK II.
CH. VI.

Great Britain at that time was a hundred and forty million pounds, and the population ten millions. Hence, as will be shown in the next Book, we get an indication of the utmost that Labour alone can produce. Now, a population of ten millions at present produces three hundred and fifty millions annually.

said, that a hundred years ago the utmost that Labour could produce in the most advanced country of Europe was *a hundred and forty million pounds* annually for a population of *ten millions*, or—let me repeat —*fourteen pounds* per head. The production per head is now *thirty-five pounds;* or, for each ten millions of population, *three hundred and fifty millions*. The point on which presently I shall insist at length is this : that if Labour is to be credited with producing the whole of the smaller sum, the entire difference between the smaller sum and the larger is to be credited to Ability operating on industry through Capital. That is to say, for every *three hundred and fifty millions* of our present national income, Labour produces only *a hundred and forty millions* whilst Ability and Capital produce *two hundred and ten*. But the fact may be put yet more clearly than this. Of our present national income of *thirteen hundred millions*, Labour produces about *five hundred*, whilst Ability and Capital produce about *eight hundred*. It could indeed be shown, as I just now indicated, that Labour in reality produces less than this, and Ability and Capital more; but for argument's sake we will let the calculation stand thus, in order that Labour shall be at all events credited with not less than its due.

And now as to Capital and Ability, and the *eight hundred millions* produced by them, what has just been said can be put in a simpler way. Capital is not only the material means through which Ability acts on and assists Labour, but it is a material means which Ability has itself created. So long as Labour alone was the principal productive agent, those vast accumulations which are distinctive of the modern world were unknown and impossible. Professor Thorold Rogers has pointed out how small was the Capital of this country at so late a date as the close of the seventeenth century. Labour alone was unable to supply a surplus from any such accumulation as we now call Capital. These became possible only by the increasing action of Ability. They were taken from the products which Ability added to the products of Labour. Capital therefore *is* Ability in a double sense —not only in the sense that as a productive

BOOK II.
CH. VI.

And it will accordingly be shown in the next Book that the whole of this increment is produced by Ability, and not by Labour.

BOOK II.
CH. VI.

agent it represents Ability, but in the sense that Ability has created it. We may therefore for the present leave Capital entirely out of our discussion, regarding it as comprehended under the term and the idea of Ability; although when we come to consider the question of distribution, we shall have to take account of the distinction between the two. But for the present we are concerned with the problem of production only; and in dealing with that part of it which alone is now before us, we have to do only with two, and not three forces—not with Labour, Ability, and Capital, but with Labour and Ability only.

The calculation, therefore, which was put forward just now may be expressed in yet simpler terms. Of our present national income of *thirteen hundred millions*, Labour produces *five hundred millions* and Ability *eight hundred*. And now comes another point which yet remains to be mentioned. When we speak of Labour, we mean not an abstract quality: what we mean is labouring men. Similarly, when we talk of Ability, we do not mean an abstract quality either: we mean men who

PRODUCT OF THE ABILITY OF THE FEW 167

possess and exercise it. But whereas when we talk of Labour we mean an immense number of men, when we talk of Ability—as I shall show presently—we mean a number that by comparison is extremely small. The real fact then on which I am here insisting, and which I shall now proceed to substantiate and explain further, is that, whilst the immense majority of the population of this country produce little more than one-third of the income, a body of men who are comparatively a mere handful actually produce little less than two-thirds of it.

BOOK III

AN EXPOSURE OF THE CONFUSIONS IMPLIED IN SOCIALISTIC THOUGHT AS TO THE MAIN AGENT IN MODERN PRODUCTION.

CHAPTER I

The Confusion of Thought involved in the Socialistic Conception of Labour.

THERE is one point which now must be quite plain to every reader, and on which there is no need to insist further; namely, that Ability is as truly a productive agent as Labour, and that if Labour produces any part of contemporary wealth, Ability just as truly produces another part. This proposition, when put in a general way, will, after what has been said, not be disputed by anybody; but there are various arguments which readers of socialistic sympathies will probably invoke as disproving it in the particular form just given to it. Certain of these arguments require to be discussed at length; but the rest can be disposed off quickly, and we will get them out of the way first. They are, indeed, not

After what has now been said, every one will admit that Ability, as distinct from Labour, is as truly a productive agent as Labour is.

so much arguments as confusions of thought, due largely to an inaccurate use of language.

These confusions are practically all comprehended in the common socialistic formula which declares all production, under modern conditions, to be what Socialists call "socialised." By this is meant that the whole wealth of the community is produced by the joint action of all the classes of men and of all the faculties employed in its production; and the formula thus includes, as Socialists will be careful to tell us, all those faculties which are here described as Ability. Now such a doctrine, if we consider its superficial sense merely, is so far from being untrue that it is a truism. But if we consider what it implies, if we consider the only meaning which gives it force as a socialistic argument, or indeed invests it with the character of any argument at all, we shall find it to be a collection of fallacies for which the truism is only a cloak. For the implied meaning is not the mere barren statement that the exertions of all contribute to the joint result, but that the exertions of all contribute to it in an equal degree; the further implication being that all therefore should share alike in it.

This is really Mill's argument with respect to Land and Labour, put into different language and applied to Labour and Ability. It says in effect precisely what was said by Mill, that when two causes are both necessary to producing a given result, it is absurd to say that the one produces more or less of it than the other: only here the argument can be used with greater apparent force. For the Socialists may say that if the principle which has been explained in this book is admitted, and if Ability is held to produce all that part of the product which is over and above what Labour could produce by itself, Labour, by the same reasoning, could be proved to produce the whole of the product, since, without the assistance of Labour, Ability could produce nothing. Accordingly, they will go on to say, this conclusion being absurd, the reasoning which leads to it must be false, and we must fall back again on the principle set forth by Mill. Labour and Ability are both necessary to the result, and being equally necessary must be held to contribute equally to producing it.

This argument, as I have said, has great apparent force; but again we have a plausi-

BOOK III. CH. I.

Making use of the same fallacy as that of Mill, which has been already criticised.

bility which is altogether upon the surface. If Labour and Ability were here conceived of as faculties, without regard to the number of men possessing them, the argument would, whatever its logical value, coincide broadly with one great practical fact, to which by and by I shall call the reader's attention; namely, that Labour and Ability do in this country divide between them the joint product in nearly equal portions. But those who make use of the socialistic formula use it with a meaning very different from the above. When they say that Ability and Labour contribute equally to producing a given amount of wealth, they mean not that the men who exercise one faculty produce collectively as much as the men who exercise the other; for that might mean that *five hundred men of Ability* produced as much as *five hundred thousand labourers;* and that is the very position which the Socialists desire to combat. They mean something which is the exact reverse of this: not that one faculty produces as much as the other faculty, but that one man produces as much as, and no more than another man, no matter which faculty he exercises in the producing process. They mean not that the faculty of Labour which an ordinary ploughman represents, produces as much as the faculty represented by an Arkwright or by a Stevenson, but that the individual ploughman, by the single task which he himself performs, adds as much to his country's wealth as the creators of the spinning-frame and the locomotive.

As soon as we realise that this is what the argument means, its apparent plausibility turns into a sort of absurdity which common sense rejects, even before seeing why it does so. We will not, however, be content with dismissing the argument as absurd: there is an idea at the back of it which requires and deserves to be examined. It is an idea which rests upon the fact already alluded to, that though Ability can make nothing without Labour, Labour can make something without Ability; and that thus the labourers who work under the direction of an able man each contribute a kind of exertion more essential to the result than he does. Each can say to him, "I am something without you. You, on the contrary, are nothing without me." Thus there arises a more or less conscious idea of Labour as a force which, if only properly organised, will be able at any moment,

BOOK III.
CH. I.

But in it there is, indeed, a plausible view as to Labour, which must be refuted, not only ridiculed. According to this view, Labour can always bring Ability to terms by refusing to exert itself.

by refusing to exert itself, to render Ability helpless, and so bring it to terms and become its master, instead of being, as now, its servant.

But this idea, which is suggested, and seems to be supported, by the modern development of labour-organisation and strikes, really ignores the most fundamental facts of the case. In the first place, it may be observed that though Ability, regarded as a faculty, is no doubt helpless unless there is Labour for it to act upon, Ability, if we take it to mean the men possessing the faculty, is, whatever happens, in as good a position as Labour; for the average man of ability can always become a labourer. But the principal point to realise is far more important than this. We are perfectly right in saying, as was said just now, that if Labour should refuse to exert itself, Ability could produce nothing; but it seems completely to escape the notice of those who use this argument that to refuse to exert itself is what Labour can never do, except for very short times, and to a quite unimportant extent; and it can only do thus much when Ability indirectly helps it. The ideas of the power of Labour which are suggested by the phenomenon of the

BOOK III. CH. I.

But Labour cannot refuse to exert itself for long, and never except with the assistance of Capital.

strike are, as I shall by and by show more fully, curiously fallacious. Men can strike—that is to say, cease to labour—only when they have some store on which to live when they are idle; and such a store is nothing but so much Capital. A strike, therefore, represents the power not of Labour, but of Capital.[1] The Capital which is available in the present day for supporting strikes would never have been in existence but for the past action of Ability; and what is still more important, a widespread strike would very quickly exhaust it. Further, a strike, no matter what Capital were at the back of it, could never be more than partial for even a single day; for there are many kinds of Labour, such as transport and distribution of food, the constant performance of which is required by even the humblest lives. But it is not necessary to dwell on such small matters as these. It is enough to point to the fact, which does not require proving—the broad fact that men, taken as a whole, can no more refuse to labour than they can refuse to breathe. What compels them

[1] This fact has been commented on with much force by Mr. Gourlay in a paper contributed by him to the *National Review*.

> BOOK III. CH. I.
>
> *Nature, not the men of ability, forces the majority of men to Labour.*

to labour is not the employing class, but Nature. The employing class—the men of ability—merely compel them to labour in a special way.

But Ability itself stands on an entirely different footing. Whereas Labour, as a whole, cannot cease to exert itself, Ability can. Indeed, for long periods of history it has hardly exerted itself at all; whilst its full industrial power, as we know it now, only began to be felt a century and a half ago. Labour, in other words, represents a necessary kind of exertion, which can always be counted on as we count on some force of Nature: Ability represents a voluntary kind of exertion, which can only be induced to manifest itself under certain special circumstances. Accordingly,

> *But Nature forces no one to exert Ability; therefore Ability is, in the long run, in a stronger position than Labour.*

whilst Labour can make no terms with Nature, Ability in the long run can always make terms with Labour. It will thus be seen that the set of arguments founded on the conception of Labour as stronger than Ability, because more necessary, are arguments founded on a complete misconception of facts. I speak of them as arguments; but they hardly deserve the name. Rather they are vague ideas that float in the minds of many people, and suggest beliefs or

THE ORGANIST AND BELLOWS-BLOWER 179

opinions to which they can give no logical basis. At all events, after what has been said, we may dismiss them from our thoughts, and turn to another fallacy that lurks in the socialistic formula.

I said of that formula that, the moment its meaning was realised, it struck the mind as an absurdity, even before the mind knew why. Let us now apply it to two simple cases, which will show its absurdity in a yet more striking manner. There is an old story commonly told of Handel. The great composer had been playing some magnificent piece of music on the organ; and as soon as the last vibration of inspired sound had subsided, he was greeted by the voice of the man who blew the bellows, saying, "I think that we two played that beautifully." "*We!*" exclaimed Handel. "What had you to do with it?" He turned again to the keys, and struck them, but not a note came. "Ha!" said the bellows-blower, "what have I to do with it? Admit that I have as much to do with it as you have, or I will not give you the power to sound a single chord." The whole point of this story lies in the fact that the argument of the bellows-blower, though

[margin: BOOK III. CH. I. Let us now test the socialistic view by examples: By the case of an organist and the man who blows the bellows;]

possessed of a certain plausibility, is at the same time obviously absurd. But according to the principles of the Socialists, it is absolutely and entirely true. It exhibits those principles applied in the most perfect way. With just the same force, it may be said about a great picture by the man who has woven the canvas, or tacked it to its wooden frame. This man may, according to the socialistic theory of production, call the picture the socialised product of the great painter and himself, and, though no more able to draw than a child of four years old, may put himself on a level with a Millais or an Alma Tadema. To the production of the result the canvas is as necessary as the painter.

The nature of the fallacy which leads us to such conclusions as these is revealed almost instantly by the light such conclusions throw on it. It consists in ignoring the fact that whilst anybody, not a cripple or idiot, can blow the bellows of an organ, or stretch the canvas for a picture, only one man in a million can make music like Handel, or cover the canvas with pictures like Millais or Alma Tadema. The nature of the situation will be understood most accurately if we imagine the bellows-blower at the key-board of the organ, and the canvas-stretcher with the painter's brushes. The one, no doubt, could elicit a large volume of sound; the other could cover the canvas with daubs of unmeaning colour. These men, then, when they work for the artists of whom we speak, may very properly be credited with a share in as much of the result as would have been produced if they had been in the artists' places. That is to say, to the production of mere sound the bellows-blower may be held to contribute as much as the great musician; and the canvas-stretcher as much as the painter to the mere laying on of colour. But all the difference between an unmeaning discord and music, all the difference between an unmeaning daub and a picture, is due to qualities that are possessed by no one except the musician and the painter.[1] The

[1] The matter may also be put in this way. There are *ninety-nine labourers* engaged on a certain work at which there is room for *a hundred*. The *ninety-nine men* produce every week value to the amount of *ninety-nine pounds*. There are two candidates for the hundredth place: one a labourer, John; and one, a man of ability, James. If John takes the vacant place, we have *a hundred men* producing *a hundred pounds*. If James takes the vacant place, the productivity of labour by his action is (we will say)

BOOK III. CH. I.

The socialistic view of production would be true only were a certain fact of life quite different to what it is.

socialistic theory of production would be true only on the supposition that the faculties employed in production were all equally common, and that everybody is equally capable of exertion of every grade. Now is this supposition true, or is it not true? A moment ago I spoke of it, assuming it to be obviously false; and many people will think it is hardly worth discussion. That, however, is far from being the case. It is a supposition which, as we have seen, lies at the very root of Socialism: the question it involves is a broad question of fact; and it is necessary, by an appeal to fact, to show that it is as false as I have assumed it to be.

The great feature in modern production is the progress in the productivity of the same number of men.

Let me once again, then, state the great proposition which I am anxious to put beyond the reach of all denial or misconception. A given number of people, a hundred years ago, produced yearly in this country *a hundred*

doubled, and we have *a hundred men* producing *a hundred and ninety-eight pounds*. No amount of theory based on the fact that James could do nothing without the *ninety-nine labourers* can obscure or do away with the practical truth and importance of the fact that the exertion of James will produce *ninety-eight pounds* more than the exertion of John; and any person with whom the decision rested, which of these two men should take the hundredth place, would base their decision on this fact.

and forty million pounds. The same number of people to-day produce two and a half times as much. Labour, a hundred years ago, could not have produced more than the total product of the community—that is to say, *a hundred and forty million pounds*; and, if it produced that then, it produces no more now. The whole added product is produced by the action of Ability. The proposition is a double one. Let us take the two parts in order.

I have already here and there pointed out in passing how certain special advances in the productive powers of the community were due demonstrably to Ability, not to Labour; but I have waited till our argument had arrived at its present stage to insist on the general truth that, except within very narrow limits, Labour is, in its very nature, not progressive at all. If we cast our eyes backwards as far into the remote past as any records or relics of human existence will carry us, we can indeed discern three steps in industrial progress, which we may, if we please, attribute to the self-development of Labour—the use of stone, the use of bronze, and the use of iron. But these steps followed each other slowly,

History shows us that Labour is not progressive, except within very narrow limits that were reached long ago, or, at all events, by the end of the last century.

and at immeasurable intervals; and though the last was taken in the early morning of history, yet Labour even then had, in certain respects, reached for thousands of years an efficiency which it has never since surpassed. In the lake-dwellings of Switzerland, which belong to the age of stone, objects have been found which bear witness to a manual skill equal to that of the most dexterous workmen of to-day. No labour, again, is more delicate than that of engraving gems; and yet the work of the finest modern gem-engravers is outdone by that of the ancient Greeks and Romans. It was even found, when the unburied ship of a Viking was being reproduced for the International Exhibition at Chicago, that in point of mere workmanship, with all our modern appliances, it was impossible to make the copy any better than the original; whilst, if we institute a comparison with times nearer our own—especially if we come to the close of the last century—it is hardly necessary to say that in every operation which depended on training of eye and hand, the great-grandfathers of the present generation were the equals of their great-grandsons.

A REMARKABLE ILLUSTRATION

We will therefore content ourselves with comparing the labourers of to-day with the labourers of the days of Pitt; and with regard to those two sets of men, we may safely say this, that in whatever respect the latter seem able to do more than the former, their seemingly increased power can be definitely and distinctly traced to some source outside themselves, from which it has been taken and lent to them—in other words, to the ability of some one able man, or else to the joint action of a body of able men. A single illustration is sufficient to prove this. It consists of a fact to which I have alluded in general terms already. It is as follows:—

When Watt had perfected his steam-engine in structure, design, and principle, and was able to make a model which was triumphantly successful in its working, he encountered an obstacle of which few people are aware, and which, had it not been overcome, would have made the development of steam-power, as we know it now, an utter impossibility. It was indeed, in the opinion of the engineer Smeaton, fatal to the success of Watt's steam-engine altogether. This obstacle was the

Book III. Ch. I. — Let us then compare the workers of that period with their great-grandsons of to-day.

difficulty of making cylinders, of any useful size, sufficiently true to keep the pistons steam-tight. Watt, with indomitable perseverance, endeavoured to train men to the degree of accuracy required, by setting them to work at cylinders, and at nothing else; and by inducing fathers to bring up their sons with them in the workshop, and thus from their earliest youth habituate them to this single task. By this means, in time, a band of labourers was secured in whom skill was raised to the highest point of which it is capable. But not even all the skill of those carefully-trained men—men trained by the greatest mechanical genius of the modern world—was equal to making cylinders approaching the standard of accuracy which was necessary to render the steam-engine, as we now know it, a possibility. But what the Labour of the cleverest labourer could never be brought to accomplish, was instantly and with ease accomplished by the action of Ability. Henry Maudsley, by introducing the slide-rest, did at a single stroke for all the mechanics in the country what Watt, after years of effort, was unable to do for any of them. The

Marginalia: BOOK III. CH. I. — We shall see that in Labour itself there has been no progress whatsoever. Ability has been the sole progressive agent.

Ability of Maudsley, congealed in this beautiful instrument, took the tool out of the hands of Labour at the turning-lathe, and held it to the surface of the cylinder, whilst Labour looked on and watched. With this iron "mate" lent to him,—this child of an alien brain,—the average mechanic was enabled to accomplish wonders which no mechanic in the world by his own skill could approach. The power of one man descended at once on a thousand workshops, and sat on each of the labourers like the fire of an industrial Pentecost; and their own personal efficiency, which was the slowly-matured product of centuries, was, by a power acting outside themselves, increased a hundredfold in the course of a few years.

Illustrations of this kind might be multiplied without limit; but nothing could add to the force of the one just given, or show more clearly how the productivity of Labour is fixed, and the power of Ability, and of Ability alone, is progressive. There is, however, a very important argument which objectors may use here with so much apparent force that, although it is entirely fallacious, it requires to be considered carefully.

There is, however, a plausible objection to this view which we must consider.

CHAPTER II

That the Ability which at any given period is a Producing Agent, is a Faculty residing in and belonging to living Men.

IT may amuse the reader to hear this argument stated—forcibly, if not very fully—by an American Socialist, in an anonymous letter to myself. I had published an article in *The North American Review*, giving a short summary of what I have said in the preceding chapters with regard to the part played by Ability in production; and the letter which I will now give was sent me as a criticism on this:

<small>The objection is thus put by an American Socialist: that it is absurd to say that</small> Sir—Your article in the current number of *The North American Review* on "Who are the Chief Wealth Producers?" in my judgment is the crowning absurdity of the various effusions that parade under the self-assumed title of political

economy. In the vulgar parlance of some newspapers, it is hog-wash. It is utterly senseless, and wholly absurd and worthless. You propose to publish a book in which you will elaborate your theory. Well, if the book has a large sale, it will not be because the author has any ability as a writer on economical subjects, but rather that the buyers are either dupes or fools. All the increase in wealth that has resulted by reason of men using ploughs was produced by the man who invented the plough —eh? The total amount of the wealth produced by men by reason of their using certain appliances in the form of tools or machines is produced by the man who invented the tool or machine—eh? perhaps some one in Egypt thousands of years ago? Such stuff is not only worthless hog-wash : it is nauseating, is worthy of the inmate of Bedlam.

Primæval inventors, such as the inventor of the plough, are still producing wealth by their ability; and if absurd in this case, then in all cases.

Now the argument implied in this charming letter, so far as it goes, is sound; and I will put it presently in a more comprehensive form. Its fault is that it goes a very little way, and does not even approach the position it is adduced to combat. To say that if one man who lived thousands of years ago could be shown to be the sole and only inventor of the plough, then all the increase of wealth that has since been produced by ploughing

BOOK III.
CH. II.

ought to be credited to the Ability of this one man, is practically no doubt as absurd[1] as the writer of the letter thinks it; and were such the result of the reasoning in this volume, it would reduce that reasoning to an absurdity.

To this there are two answers. The first is that the simpler inventions are probably due, not to Ability at all, but to the common experience of the average man;

That reasoning, however, leads to no result of the kind; and it is necessary to explain to the reader exactly why it fails to do so. It fails to do so because ploughs, and other implements equally simple, instead of representing those conditions of production to which alone the reasoning in this volume applies, represent conditions which are altogether opposed to them. The plough, or at least such a plough as was in use in ancient Egypt, is the very type and embodiment of the non-progressive nature of Labour, as opposed to, and contrasted with, the progressive nature of Ability. The plough, indeed, in its simplest form, was probably not the result of Ability at all, but rather of the experience of multitudes of common men, acting on the intelligence which common

[1] I say *practically* as absurd, meaning absurd and practically meaningless in an economic argument. There are many points of view from which it would be philosophically true.

men possess; just as, even more obviously, was the use of a stick to walk with, or of a flail for thrashing corn. It will perhaps, however, be said that in that case, according to the definition given by me, the plough would be the result of Ability all the same, only that it would prove Ability to be a faculty almost as universal as Labour. And no doubt it would prove this of Ability of a low kind; indeed, we may admit that it does prove it. Everybody has a little Ability in him, just as everybody has a little poetry; but in cases of this kind everything is a question of degree; and for practical purposes we are compelled to classify men not according to faculties which, strictly speaking, they possess, but according to the degree in which they possess them. Cold, strictly speaking, is merely a low degree of heat; but for all practical purposes winter is opposed to summer. Similarly, a man who has just enough poetry in him to be able—as most men can—to scribble a verse of doggerel, is for all practical purposes opposed to a Shakespeare or a Dante; and similarly also the man who has just enough Ability in him to discover the use of a stick, a flail, or a plough, is for all practical purposes opposed to the men who are capable of inventing implements of a higher and more complicated order. Nor is the line which we thus draw drawn arbitrarily. It is a line drawn for us by the whole industrial history of mankind; and never was there a division more striking and more persistent. For the simpler implements in question, from the first days when they were invented,—" thousands of years ago," as my American correspondent says,—remained what they then were up to the beginning of the modern epoch; and in many countries, such as India, they remain the same to-day. The simpler industrial arts, then, and the simpler implements of industry are sharply marked off from the higher and more complicated by the fact that, whilst the latter are demonstrably due to individuals, have flourished only within the area of their influence, and have constituted a sudden and distinct advance on the former, the former have apparently been due to the average faculties of mankind, and have remained practically unchanged from the days of their first dis-

A MORE IMPORTANT POINT 193

covery. Accordingly, the distinction between the two being so marked and enormous, the faculties to which they are respectively due, even if differing only in degree, yet differ in degree so much that they are for practical purposes different faculties, and must be called by different names. The simple inventions, then, to which my correspondent refers, together with the wealth produced by them, are to be credited to Labour, the non-progressive character of which they embody and represent, and have nothing to do with that Ability which is the cause of industrial progress.

My correspondent's letter, however, whether he saw it himself or not, really raises a point far more important than this. For even if the invention of the plough had been the work of one man only, if it had involved as much knowledge and genius as the invention of the steam-engine, and if, but for this one man, ploughs would never have existed, yet to attribute to the Ability of this one man all the wealth that has been subsequently produced by ploughing would still be practically as absurd as my correspondent implies it would be.

BOOK III. CH. II.

But even if invented by Ability, we should still attribute the wealth now produced by them to Labour;

BOOK III.
CH. II.
———
Because the commonest labourer, when once he has seen them, can make and use them.

Now why is this? The reason why is as follows. Although, according to such an hypothesis, if a plough had not been made by this one able man, no ploughs would ever have been made by anybody, yet when such a simple implement has once been made and used, anybody who has seen it can make and use others like it; so that the Ability of the inventor of the plough increases the productivity of every labourer who uses it, not by co-operating with him, but by actually passing into him. Thus, so far as this particular operation is concerned, the simplest labourer becomes endowed with all the powers of the inventor; and the inventor thenceforward is, in no practical sense, the producer of the increased product of what he has enabled the labourer to produce, any more than a father is the producer of what is produced by his son.

And if the productivity of Labour were increased by inventions alone, and if all inventions were as simple as the primæval plough—if, when once seen, anybody were able to make them, and, having once made them, to use them to the utmost advantage— then, though Ability might still be the sole cause of every fresh addition to the productive powers of exertion, these added powers would be all made over to Labour, and be absorbed and appropriated by it, just as Lear's kingdom was made over to his daughters; and whatever increased wealth might be produced thenceforward through their agency would be the true product of Labour, which had in itself become more effective. But, as a matter of fact, this is not the case; and it is not so for two reasons. In the first place, such implements as the primæval plough differ from the implements on which modern industry depends, in the complexity alike of their structure, and of the principles involved in it; so that without the guidance of Ability of many kinds, Labour alone would be powerless to reproduce them; and, in the second place, as these implements multiply, not only is Ability more and more necessary for their manufacture, but is more and more necessary also for the use of them when manufactured. One of the principal results of the modern development of machinery, or of the use, by new processes, of newly discovered powers of Nature, is the increasing division and sub-

But the inventions by which Ability in the modern world has increased production are the very opposite of these inventions of earlier days; for they require as much Ability to use them to the best advantage as they required to make them.

BOOK III.
CH. II.

division of Labour; so that the labourers, as I have said before, by the introduction of this mass of machinery, become themselves the most complicated machine of all, each labourer being a single minute wheel, and Ability being the framework which alone keeps them in their places. It may be said, therefore, that each modern invention or discovery by which the productivity of human exertion is increased has upon Labour an effect exactly opposite to that which was produced on it by such inventions as the primæval plough. Instead of making Labour more efficacious in itself, they make it less and less efficacious, unless it is assisted by Ability.

They do not become, as is vulgarly said, common property. They belong to those who can use them;

And here we have the answer to the real argument which lies at the bottom of my American correspondent's letter—an argument which, in some such words as the following, is to be found repeated in every Socialistic treatise: "When once an invention is made, it becomes common property." So it does in a certain theoretical sense; but only in the sense in which a knowledge of Chinese becomes common property in England on the publication of a Chinese grammar. For all practical purposes, such a statement is about as true as to say that because anybody can buy a book on military tactics, everybody is possessed of the genius of the Duke of Wellington. The real truth is, that to utilise modern inventions, and to maintain the conditions of industry which these inventions subserve, as much Ability is required as was required to invent them; though, as I shall have occasion to point out later on, the Ability is of a different kind.

These considerations bring us to another important point, which must indeed from the beginning have been more or less obvious, but which must now be stated explicitly. That point is, that when we speak of Ability as producing at any given time such and such a portion of the national income, as distinguished from the portion which is produced by Labour, we are speaking of Ability possessed by living men, who possess it either in the form of their own superior faculties, assimilating, utilising, and adding to the inventions and discoveries of their predecessors; or in the form of inherited Capital, which those predecessors

And more and more is living Ability required to maintain and use the powers left to it by the Ability of the past.

We must, then, here note that when Ability is said to produce so much of the national income, what is meant is the Ability of men alive at the time, have produced and left to them. Thus, though dead men like Arkwright, or Watt, or Stevenson may, in a certain theoretical sense, be considered as continuing to produce wealth still, they cannot be considered to do so in any sense that is practical; because they cannot as individuals put forward any practical claims, or influence the situation any further by their actions. For all practical purposes, then, their Ability as a productive force exists only in those living men who inherit or give effect to its results. Now, of the externalised or congealed Ability which is inherited in the form of Capital, as distinguished from the personal Ability by which Capital is utilised, we need not speak here, though we shall have to do so presently. For this inherited Capital would not only be useless in production, but would actually disappear and evaporate like a lump of camphor, if it were not constantly used, and, in being used, renewed, by that personal Ability which inherits it, and is inseparable from the living individual; and, though it will be necessary to consider Capital apart from this when we come to deal with the problem of distribution,

THE ABILITY OF LIVING MEN

all that we need consider when we are dealing with the problem of production is this personal Ability, which alone makes Capital live.

So far, then, as modern production is concerned, all the results of past Ability, instead of becoming the common property of Labour, become on the whole, with allowance for many exceptions, more and more strictly the monopoly of living Ability; because these results becoming more and more complicated, Ability becomes more and more essential to the power of mastering and of using them. As, however, I shall point out by and by, in more than one connection, the Ability that masters and uses them differs much in kind from the Ability that originally produced them: one difference being that, whereas to invent and perfect some new machine requires Ability of the highest class in, let us say, one man, and Ability of the second class in a few other men, his partners; to use this machine to the best advantage, and control and maintain the industry which its use has inaugurated or developed, may require perhaps Ability of only the second class in one man,

Who are practically the monopolists not only of their own special powers, but of the complicated discoveries of their predecessors.

BOOK III. CH. II.

And the monoply of Ability grows stricter at each fresh stage of progress.

but will require Ability of the third and fourth class in a large number of men.

Ability therefore—the Ability of living men—constantly tends, as the income of the nation grows, to play a larger part in its production, or to produce a larger part of it; whilst Labour, though without it no income could be produced at all, tends to produce a part which is both relatively and absolutely smaller. We assume, for instance, that the Labour of this country a hundred years ago was capable of producing the whole of what was the national income then. If it could by itself, without any Ability to guide it, have succeeded then, when production was so much simpler, in just producing the yearly amount in question,—which, as a matter of fact, it could not have done even then,—the same amount of Labour, without any Ability to guide it, could certainly not succeed in producing so much now, when all the conditions of production have become so much more complicated, and when elaborate organisation is necessary to make almost any effort effective.

Thus the argument above quoted against the claims of

Thus the argument, which was fermenting

THE PRODUCTIVITY OF ABILITY

in my American correspondent's mind, and which he regarded as reducing the claims of Ability to "hog-wash," really affords the means, if examined carefully and minutely, of establishing yet more firmly the position it was invoked to shatter, and of making the claims of Ability not only clearer but more extensive.

BOOK III.
CH. II.
———
Ability, when examined, only throws additional light on their strength.

CHAPTER III

That Ability is a natural Monopoly, due to the congenital Peculiarities of a Minority. The Fallacies of other Views exposed.

<small>But the Socialists have yet another fallacy with which they will attempt to neutralise the force of what has just been said.</small>

BUT the socialistic theorist will not even yet have been silenced. Even if he is constrained to admit the truth of all that has just been said, we shall find that he still possesses in his arsenal of error another set of arguments by which he will endeavour to do away with its force. These are generally presented to us in mere loose rhetorical forms; but however loosely they may be expressed, they contain a distinct meaning, which I will endeavour to state as completely and as clearly as is possible.

<small>They will say that Ability is the creation of special opportunity, and</small>

Put shortly, it is as follows. Though Ability and Labour may both be productive faculties, and though it may be allowed that the one is more productive than the other, it is on the whole a mere matter of social accident—a matter depending on station, fortune, and education—which faculty is exercised by this or that individual. Thus, though it may be allowed that a great painter and the man who stretches his canvas, or an inventor like Watt and the average mechanic who works for him, do, by the time that both are mature men, differ enormously in the comparative efficacy of their faculties, yet the difference is mainly due to circumstances posterior to their birth; that the circumstances which developed the higher faculties in one man might equally well have developed them in the other; and that the circumstances in question, even if only a few can profit by them, are really created by the joint action of the many.

BOOK III.
CH. III.
—
that everybody at birth is potentially an able man.

The above contention contains several different propositions, which we will presently examine one by one. We will, however, take its general meaning first. One of the chief exponents of this, strange as the fact may seem, is that vehement anti-Socialist, Mr. Herbert Spencer. Mr. Spencer disposes of the claims of the man of ability as a force distinct from the generation at large to which he belongs, by saying that "Before the great man can

BOOK III. CH. III.

This is sometimes expressed in saying that "the great man is made by his age," i.e. by the opportunities others have secured for him.

remake his society, his society must make him." Thus, to take an example from art, the genius of a man like Shakespeare is explained by reference to the condition of the civilised world, and of England more especially, during the reign of Queen Elizabeth. The temper of the human mind caused by centuries of Catholicism, the stir of the human mind shown in the Reformation or the Renaissance, and the sense of the new world then being conquered in America, are all dwelt on as general or social causes which produced in an individual poet a greatness which has been since unequalled.

But this, though true psychologically, is absolutely false in the practical sphere of economics.

Now this reasoning, if used to combat a certain psychological error, no doubt expresses a very important truth; but if it is transferred to the sphere of economics its whole meaning vanishes. It was originally used in opposition to the now obsolete theory according to which a genius was a kind of spiritual aerolite, fallen from heaven, and related in no calculable way to its environment. It was used, for instance, to prove with regard to Shakespeare that had he lived in another age he would have thought and written differently, and that he might have been a worse poet under circumstances less exciting to the imagination. But when we leave the psychological side of the case, and look at its practical side, a set of facts is forced on us which are of quite a different order. We are forced to reflect that though Shakespeare's mind may have been what it was because the age acted on it, the age was acting on all Shakespeare's contemporaries, and yet it produced one Shakespeare only. If Queen Elizabeth had been told that it was the age which produced Shakespeare, and in consequence had ordered that three or four more Shakespeares should be brought to her, her courtiers, do what they would, would have been unable to find them; and the reason is plain. The age acts on, or sets its stamp on, the character of every single mind that belongs to it; but the effect in each case depends on the mind acted on; and it is only one mind amongst ordinary minds innumerable, that this universal action can fashion into a great poet. And what is true of poetic genius is true of industrial Ability. The great director of Labour is as rare as a great poet is; and though Ability of lower degrees is far commoner than

BOOK III.
CH. III.

Ability of the highest, yet the fact that it is the age which elicits and conditions its activities does nothing to make it commoner than it would be otherwise, nor affects the fact that its possessors are relatively a small minority. For the psychologist, the action of the age is an all-important consideration; for the economist, it is a consideration of no importance at all.

But it is by no means my intention to dismiss the Socialistic argument with this simple demonstration of the irrelevance of its general meaning. I am going to call the attention of the reader to the particular meanings that are attached to it, and show how absolutely false these are, by comparing them with historical facts.

Again, Socialists urge that no perfected invention is the work of a single man, but that many men have always co-operated to produce it.

In the first place, then, the claims of the age, or of society as a whole, to be the author of industrial progress, in opposition to the claims of a minority, are supported by many writers on the ground that no invention or discovery is in reality the work of any single man. Such writers delight to multiply—and they can do so without difficulty—instances of how the most important machines or processes have been perfected only after a long lapse of time, by the efforts of many men following or co-operating with one another. Thus the electric telegraph, and the use of gas for lighting, were not the discoveries of those who first introduced them to the public; and Stevenson described the locomotive as the "invention of no one man, but of a race of mechanical engineers." Further, it is frequently urged that the same discoveries and inventions are arrived at in different places, by different minds, simultaneously; and this fact is put forward as a conclusive proof and illustration of how society, not the individual, is the true discoverer and inventor. But these arguments leave out of sight entirely the fact that, in the first place, the whole body of individuals spoken of—such as the race of engineers who produced the locomotive, or the astronomers in different countries who are discovering the same new star—form a body which is infinitesimally small itself; and secondly, that even the body of persons they represent,—namely, all of those who are engaged in the same pursuits, and have even so much as attempted any step in industrial progress,—though numerous in comparison with those who have actually succeeded in

This is true; but the class of men referred to is that very minority who are the monopolists of Ability. It is this class only, not the community in general.

BOOK III.
CH. III.

taking one, are merely a handful when compared with society as a whole, and instead of representing society, offer the strongest contrast to it. The nature of the assistance which Ability gives to Ability is an interesting question, but it is nothing to the point here. To prove that progress is the joint product of Ability and Ability, does not form a proof, but on the contrary a disproof of the proposition, that it is the joint product of Ability and Labour—or, in other words, that it is the product of the age, or the entire community.

Further, Socialists contend that Ability is the product of education, and that an equal education would equalise faculties.

The socialistic theorist, however, even if he admits the above answer, will by no means admit that it is fatal to his own position. He will still take refuge in the proposition already alluded to, that the Ability of individuals is the child of opportunity, and that Ability is rarer than Labour, and able men are a minority, only because, under existing social circumstances, the opportunities which enable it to develop itself are comparatively few. And if he is pressed to say what these opportunities are, he will say that they may be described generally by the one word education. This argument can be answered in one way only, namely, an appeal to facts; and it is hard to conceive of anything which facts more conclusively disprove. Indeed, of much industrial Ability, it can not only be shown to be false, but it is also, on the very surface of it, absurd. It is plausible as applied to Ability of one kind only, namely, that of the inventor or the discoverer; but this, as we shall see presently, is so far from being Ability as a whole, that it is not even the most important part of it. Let us, however, suppose it to be the whole for a moment, and ask how far the actual facts of life warrant us in regarding it as the child of opportunity and education. Let us first refer to that general kind of experience which is recorded in the memory of everybody who has ever been at a school or college, and which, in the lives of tutors and masters, is repeated every day. Let a hundred individuals from childhood be brought up in the same school, let them all be devoted to the study of the same branch of knowledge, let them enjoy to the fullest what is called "equality of opportunity," and it will be found that not only is there no equality in the amount of knowledge they acquire, but that there is hardly any resemblance in the uses to which they will be able to put it. Two youths may have worked together in one laboratory. One will never do more than understand the discoveries of others. The other will discover, like Columbus, some new world of mysteries. Indeed, equality of opportunity, as all experience shows, instead of tending to make the power of all men equal, does but serve to exhibit the extent to which they differ.

But particular facts are more forcible than general facts. Let us consider the men who, as a matter of history, have achieved by their Ability the greatest discoveries and inventions, and let us see if it can be said of these men, on the whole, that their Ability has been due to any exceptional education or opportunity. Speaking generally, the very reverse is the case. If education means education in the branch of work or knowledge in which the Ability of the able man is manifested, the greatest inventors of the present century have had no advantages of educational opportunity at all. Dr. Smiles observes that our greatest mechanical inventors did not even have the advantage of being brought up as engineers. "Watt," he

Marginalia: BOOK III. CH. III. — But this wild theory is in absolute opposition to the most notorious facts; As may be seen by a glance at the lives of some of the most distinguished inventors of the world.

writes, "was a mathematical instrument-maker; Arkwright was a barber; Cartwright, the inventor of the power-loom, was a clergyman; Bell, who afterwards invented the reaping-machine, was a Scotch minister; Armstrong, the inventor of the hydraulic engine, was a solicitor; and Wheatstone, inventor of the electric telegraph, was a maker of musical instruments." That knowledge is necessary to mechanical invention is of course a self-evident truth; and the acquistion of knowledge, however acquired, is education: education, therefore, was necessary to the exercise of the Ability of all these men. But the point to observe is, that they had none of them any special educational opportunity; they were placed at no advantage as compared with any of their fellows; many of them, indeed, were at a very marked disadvantage; and though, when opportunity is present, Ability will no doubt profit by it, the above examples show, and the whole course of industrial history shows,[1] that Ability is so far from being the

[1] The examples given above might be multiplied indefinitely. Maudsley was brought up as a "powder-boy" at Woolwich. The inventors of the planing machine, Clements

BOOK III. CH. III.

The theory is still further refuted by the fact that moral Ability is a matter of character and temperament, rather than of intellect.

creature of opportunity, that it is, on the contrary, in most cases the creator of it.

The mental power, however, which is exercised by the inventor and discoverer, as I have said, is but one kind of industrial Ability out of many. Ability—or the faculty by which one man assists the Labour of an indefinite number of men—consists in what may be called exceptional gifts of character, quite as much as in exceptional gifts of intellect. A sagacity, an instinctive quickness in recognising the intellect of others, a strength of will that sometimes is almost brutal, and will force a way for a new idea, like a pugilist forcing himself through a crowd, these are faculties quite as necessary as intellect for giving effect to what intellect discovers or creates; and they do not always, or even generally, reside in the same individuals. The genius which is capable of grappling with ideas and principles, and in the domain of thought will display the sublimest daring,

and Fox, were brought up, the one as a slater, the other as a domestic servant. Neilson, the inventor of the hot-blast, was a millwright. Roberts, the inventor of the self-acting mule and the slotting-machine, was a quarryman. The illustrious Bramah began life as a common farm-boy.

often goes with a temperament of such social timidity as to unfit its possessor for facing and dealing with the world. It is one thing to perfect some new machine or process, it is another to secure Capital which may put it into practical operation; and again, if we put the difficulty of securing Capital out of the question by supposing the inventor to be a large capitalist himself, there is another difficulty to be considered, more important far than this—the difficulty dealt with in the last chapter—namely, the conduct of the business when once started. Here we come to a number of complicated tasks, in which the faculty of invention or discovery offers no assistance whatsoever. We come to tasks which have to do, not with natural principles, but with men—the thousand tasks of daily and of hourly management. A machine or process is invented by intellect—there is one step. It is put into practical operation with the aid of Capital—there is another. When these two steps are taken, they do not require to be repeated, but the tasks of management are tasks which never cease; on the contrary, as has been said already, they tend rather to become ever more numerous and complicated. Nor do they consist only of the mere management of labourers, the selection of foremen and inspectors, and the minutiæ of industrial discipline. They consist also of what may be called the policy of the whole business — the quick comprehension of the fluctuating wants of the consumer, the extent to which these may be led, the extent to which they must be followed, the constant power of adjusting the supply of a commodity to the demand. On the importance of these faculties there is a great deal to be said; but I will only observe here that it is embodied and exemplified in the fact that successful inventors and discoverers are nearly always to be found in partnership with men who are not inventors, but who are critics of inventions, who understand how to manage and use them, and who supplement the Ability that consists of gifts of intellect by that other kind of Ability that consists of gifts of character.

Now if, as we have seen, it is entirely contrary to experience to suppose that inventive Ability is produced by educational opportunity, much more is it contrary to experience —it is contrary even to common sense—to suppose that Ability of character can be produced in the same way. Education, as applied to the rousing and the training of the intellect, is like a polishing process applied to various stones, which may give to all of them a certain kind of smoothness, but brings to light their differences far more than their similarity. Education may make all of us write equally good grammar, but it will not make all of us write equally good poetry, any more than cutting and polishing will turn a pebble into an emerald. And if this is true of education applied to intellect, of education applied to character it is truer still. Character consists of such qualities as temperament, strength of will, imagination, perseverance, courage; and it is as absurd to expect that the same course of education will make a hundred boys equally brave or imaginative, as it is to expect that it will make them equally tall or heavy, or decorate all of them with hair of the same colour.

Ability, then, is rare as compared with Labour, not because the opportunities are

BOOK III.
CH. III.

Equality of education and opportunity, instead of equalising characters, displays their differences.

Ability, then, is a natural monopoly; because few people are born with it.

And now let us again compare its action with that of the mass of men surrounding it.

rare which are favourable or necessary to its development, but because the minds and characters are rare which can turn opportunity to account. And now let us turn again to the more general form of the Socialistic fallacy—the general proposition that the Age, or Society, or the Human Race is the true inventor, and let us test this by a new order of facts.

I have already alluded to the stress laid by Socialists on the fact that different individuals in different parts of the world often make the same discoveries at almost the same time; and I pointed out that whatever this might teach us, applied only to a small minority of persons, and had no reference whatever to the great mass of the race. But Socialists very frequently put their view in a form even more exaggerated than that which I thus criticised. They use language which implies that the whole mass of society moves forward together at the same intellectual pace; and that discoverers and inventors merely occupy the position of persons who chance to be walking a few paces in advance of the crowd, and who thus light upon new processes or machines like so many nuggets lying and glittering on the ground, which those who follow would have presently discovered for themselves; or, again, they are represented as persons who are merely the first to utter some word or exclamation which is already on the lips of everybody. Let us, then, take the three great elements which go to make up the industrial prosperity of this country—the manufacture of iron, the manufacture of cotton, and the development of the steam-engine, and see how far the history of each of these lends any support to the theory just mentioned.

We will begin with the manufacture of iron. Ever since man was acquainted with the use of this metal till a time removed from our own by a few generations only, its production from the ore was dependent entirely upon wood, which alone of all fuels—so far as knowledge then went—had the chemical qualities necessary for the process of smelting. The iron industry in this country was therefore, till very recently, confined to wooded districts, such as parts of Sussex and Shropshire; and so large, during the seventeenth

BOOK III. CH. III.

Do able men in any sense represent the tendencies and intelligence of their average contemporaries? Let us turn for an answer to the history of the three chief industrial triumphs of this country: (1) the iron manufacture, (2) the cotton manufacture, (3) the steam-engine.

The modern development of the iron industry dependent on the use of coal in place of wood.

century, was the consumption of trees and brushwood, that the smelting furnace came to be considered by many statesmen as the destroyer of wood, rather than as the producer of metal. This view, indeed, can hardly be called exaggerated; for by the beginning of the century following the wood available for the furnaces was becoming so fast exhausted that the industry had begun to dwindle; and but for one great discovery it would have soon been altogether extinguished. This was the method of smelting iron with coal. Now to what cause was this discovery due? The answer can be given with the utmost completeness and precision. It was due to the Ability of a few isolated individuals, whose relation to their contemporaries and to their age we will now briefly glance at.

The first of these was a certain Dud Dudley, who procured a patent in the year 1620 for smelting iron ore "with coal, in furnaces with bellows"; and his process was so far successful, that at length from a single furnace he produced for a time seven tons of iron weekly. For reasons, however, which will be mentioned presently, Dudley's invention died with himself; and for fifty years after his death the application of coal to smelting was as much a lost art as it would have been had he never lived. Between the years 1718 and 1735 it was again discovered by a father and son—the Darbys of Coalbrookdale. A further step, and one of almost equal importance, was achieved by two of their foremen—brothers of the name of Cranege—assisted by Reynolds, who had married the younger Darby's daughter, and this was the application of coal to the process which succeeds smelting, namely, the conversion of crude iron into bar-iron, or iron that is malleable. Other inventors might be mentioned by whom these men were assisted, but it will be quite enough to consider the case of these. As related to the age, as related to the society round him, the one thing most striking in the life of each of them is not that he represented that society, but that he was in opposition to it, and had to fight a way for his inventions through neglect, ridicule, and persecution. The nation at large was absolutely ignorant of the very nature of the objects which these men had in view; whilst the ironmasters of the day, as a body, though not equally ignorant, disbelieved that the objects were practicable until they were actually accomplished. It is true that these great inventors were not alone in their efforts; for where they succeeded, others attempted and failed: but these failures do but show in a stronger light how rare and how great were the faculties which success demanded.

<small>The details of whose several lives are signal illustrations of what has just been said.</small>

Let us take each case separately. Dudley's life as an ironmaster was one long succession of persecution at the hands of his brothers in the trade. They petitioned the king to put a stop to his manufacture; they incited mobs to destroy his bellows and his furnaces; they harrassed him with law-suits, ruined him with legal expenses; they succeeded at last in having him imprisoned for debt; and by thus crippling the inventor, they at last killed his invention. It is true that meanwhile a few men—a very few—believed in his ideas, and attempted to work them out independently; and amongst these was Oliver Cromwell himself. He and certain partners protected themselves with a patent for the purpose, and actually bought up the works of the ruined Dudley; but all their attempts ended in utter failure. Two more adventurers, named Copley and Proger, were successively granted patents during the reign of Charles II. for this same purpose, and likewise failed ignominiously. One man alone in the whole nation had proved himself capable of accomplishing this new conquest for industry; whilst the nation as a whole, and the masters of the iron trade in particular, remained as they were—stationary in their old invincible ignorance. The two Darbys, the two Craneges, and Reynolds, though not encountering, as Dudley did, the hostility of their contemporaries, yet achieved their work without the slightest encouragement or assistance from them. The younger Darby, solitary as Columbus on his quarter-deck, watched all night by his furnace as he was bringing his process to perfection. His workmen, like the sailors of Columbus, obeyed their orders blindly; and in hardly a brain but his own did there exist the smallest consciousness that one man was laying, in secret, the foundation of his country's greatness. With regard to Reynolds and the Craneges, who imitated, though they did not perfect, the further use of coal for the production of iron that is malleable, we have similar evidence that is yet more circumstantial. Reynolds distinctly declares in a letter written to a friend that the conception of this process was so entirely original with the Craneges that it had never for a moment occurred to himself as being possible, and that they had had to convince him that it was so, against his own judgment. But when once his conversion was completed, he united his Ability with theirs; and within a very short time the second great step in our iron industry had been taken triumphantly by these three unaided men.

Were it necessary, and would space permit of it, we might extend this history further. We might cite the inventions of Huntsman, of Onions, of Cort, and Neilson, and show how each of these was conceived, was perfected, and was brought into practical use, whilst the nation as a whole remained inert, passive, and ignorant, and the experts of the trade were hostile, and sometimes equally ignorant. Huntsman perfected his process in a secrecy as carefully guarded as that of a mediæval necromancer hiding himself from the vigilance of the Church; whilst James Neilson, the inventor of the hot-blast, had at first to encounter the united ridicule and hostility of all the shrewdest and most experienced ironmasters in the kingdom.

The history of the cotton manufacture offers precisely similar evidence. Almost every one of those great improvements made in it, by which Ability has multiplied the power of Labour, had to be forced by the able men on the acceptance of adverse contemporaries. Hay was driven from the country; Hargreaves from his native town; Arkwright's mill, near Chorley, was burnt down by a mob; Peel, who used Arkwright's machinery, was at one time in danger of his life. Nor was it only the hostility of the ignorant that the inventors had to encounter. They had to conquer Capital before they could conquer Labour; for the Capitalists at the beginning were hardly more friendly to them than the labourers. The first Capitalists who assisted Arkwright, and had Ability enough to discover some promise in his invention, had not enough Ability to see their way through certain difficulties, and withdrew their help from him at the most critical moment. The enterprising men who at last became his partners, and with the aid of whose Capital his invention became successful, represented their age just as little as Arkwright did. He and they, indeed, had the same opportunities as the society round them; but they stand contrasted to the society by the different use they made of them.

<small>Also the history of the steam-engine, as a very curious anecdote will show.</small>

And now, lastly, let us come to the history of the steam-engine. We need not go over ground we have already trodden, and prove once more that in this case, as in the others, the age, in the sense of the majority of the community, had as little to do with the work of the great inventors as Hannibal had to do with the beheading of Charles I. It will be enough to insist on the fact that the scientific minority amongst whom the inventors lived, and who were busied with the same pursuits, were, as a body, concerned in it just as little. The whole forward movement, the step after step of discovery by which the power of steam has become what it now is, was due to individuals—to a minority of a minority; and this smaller minority was so far from representing the larger, or from merely marching a few steps ahead of it, that the large minority always hung back incredulous, till, in spite of itself, it was converted by the accomplished miracle. One example is enough to illustrate this. Watt, when he was perfecting his steam-engine, was in partnership with Dr. Roebuck, who advanced the money required to patent the invention, and whose energy and encouragement helped him over many practical difficulties. When the engine was almost brought to completion, Roebuck found himself so much embarrassed for money, on account of expense incurred by him in an entirely different enterprise, that he was forced to sell a large part of his property; and amongst other things with which he parted was his interest in Watt's patent. This he transferred to the celebrated engineer Boulton; and the patent for that invention which has since revolutionised the world was valued by Roebuck's creditors at only one farthing.

<small>BOOK III.
CH. III.</small>

These facts speak plainly enough for themselves; and the conscience of most men will add its own witness to what they teach us—which is this. So far as industrial progress is concerned, the majority of mankind are passive. They labour as the conditions into which they are <small>The average man, if cross-examined at the Day of Judgment, would be forced to give his testimony</small>

born compel them to labour; but they do nothing, from their cradle to their grave, so to alter these conditions that their own labour, or Labour generally, shall produce larger or improved results. The most progressive race in the world—or in other words the English race—has progressed as it has done only because it has produced the largest minority of men fitted to lead, and has been quickest in obeying their orders; but apart from these men it has had no appreciable tendency to move. Let the average Englishman ask himself if this is not absolutely true. Let him imagine himself arraigned before the Deity at the Day of Judgment, and the Deity saying this to him: "You found when you entered the world that a man's labour on the average produced each year such and such an amount of wealth. Have you done anything to make the product of the same labour greater? Have you discovered or applied any new principle to any branch of industry? Have you guided industry into any new direction? Have the exertions of any other human being been made more efficacious owing to your powers of invention, of enterprise, or of management?" There is not one man in a hundred who, if thus questioned at the Judgment-seat, would be able, on examining every thought and deed of his life, to give the Judge any answer but, "No. So far as I am concerned, the powers of Labour are as I found them."

CHAPTER IV

The Conclusion arrived at in the preceding Book restated. The Annual Amount produced by Ability in the United Kingdom.

<small>The more, then, that we examine the question, the more clearly do we see the magnitude of the work performed by Ability of the few.</small>

IN spite, then, of the arguments which Socialists have borrowed from psychology, and with which, by transferring them to the sphere of economics, and so depriving them of all practical meaning, they have contrived to confuse the problem of industrial progress, the facts of the case, when examined from a practical point of view, stand out hard and clear and unambiguous. Industrial progress is the work not of society as a whole but of a small part of it, to the entire exclusion of the larger part; the reason of this being that the faculties to which this progress is due—the faculties which I have included under the name of Industrial Ability—are found to exist only in a small percentage of individuals, and are practically absent from the minds, characters, and temperaments of the majority of the human race. Ability is, in fact, a narrow natural monopoly.

Ability, however, is of different kinds and grades, some kinds being far commoner than others; and before summing up what has been said in this chapter, it will be well to give the reader some more or less definite idea of the numerical proportion which, judging by general evidence, the men of Ability bear to the mass of labourers. Such evidence, not indeed very exact, but still corresponding broadly to the underlying facts of the case, is to be found in the number of men paying income-tax on business incomes, as compared with the number of wage-earners whose incomes escape that tax; in the number of men, that is, who earn more than *one hundred and fifty pounds* a year, as compared with the number of men who do not earn so much. It may seem at first sight that this division is purely arbitrary; but we shall see, on consideration, that it is not so. We shall find that, allowing for very numerous exceptions, men in this country do as a rule

BOOK III.
CH. IV.

But it must not be supposed that Ability is rarer than it is.

BOOK III.
CH. IV.

A rough indication of the number of able men in this country is found in the incomes earned that are above the average wages of Labour.

receive less than *one hundred and fifty pounds* a year for Labour, and that when they receive for their exertions a larger income than this they receive it for the direction of Labour, or for the exercise of some sort of Ability. Now if we take the males who are over sixteen years. of age, and who are actually engaged in some industrial occupation, we shall find that those who earn more than *one hundred and fifty pounds* a year form of the entire number something like six per cent. We may therefore say that out of every thousand men there are, on an average, sixty who are distinctly superior to their fellows, who each add more to the gross amount of the product by directing Labour, than any one man does by labouring, and who possesses Ability

The highest Ability very rare. Of all grades of Ability below the highest, there is always a plentiful supply.

to a greater or less extent. The commoner kinds of Ability, however, depend as a rule on the higher kinds, and are efficacious only as working under their direction; and if we continue our estimate on the basis we have just adopted, and accept the amount that a man makes in industry as being on the whole an evidence of the amount of his Ability, we consider that, all allowance being made for mere luck or speculation, a business income of *fifty thousand pounds* means, as a rule, Ability of the first class, of *fifteen thousand pounds* Ability of the second, and *five thousand pounds* Ability of the third, we shall find that men possessing these higher degrees of the faculty are, in comparison to the mass of employed males, very few indeed. We shall find that Ability of the third class is possessed by but one man out of two thousand; of the second class by but one man out of four thousand; and of the first class by but one man out of a hundred thousand. This is, as I have said, a very rough method of calculation, but it is not a random one; and there is reason to believe that it affords us an approximation to truth. At all events, taking it as a whole, it does not err by making Ability too rare; and we shall be certainly within the mark if, taking Ability as a whole, and waiving the question of its various classes and their rarity, we say that of the men in this country actively engaged in production, the men of Ability constitute one-sixteenth.

And now we are in a position to repeat with more precision and confidence the conclu-

BOOK III. CH. IV.

We may now repeat the conclusions arrived at in the last Book, that Ability produces at least eight-thirteenths of the present income of this country; and Labour, at the utmost, five-thirteenths.

sion which we reached at the end of the last chapter. It was there pointed out that of our present national income, consisting as it does of about *thirteen hundred million pounds*, Labour demonstrably produced not more than *five hundred million pounds*, whilst *eight hundred million pounds* at least was demonstrably the product of Ability. In the present chapter, I have substantiated that proposition: I have exposed the confusions and fallacies which have been used to obscure its truth; I have shown that Ability and Labour are two distinct forces, in the sense that whilst the latter represents a faculty common to all men, the possession of the former is the natural monopoly of the few; that the labourer and the man of Ability play such different parts in production that a given amount of wealth is no more their joint product than a picture is the joint product of a great painter and a canvas-stretcher; and I have now pointed to some rough indication of the respective numbers of the men of Ability and of the labourers. Instead, therefore, of contenting ourselves with the general statement that Ability makes so much of the national income, and Labour so much, we may say that ninety-six per cent of the producing classes produce little more than a third of our present national income, and that a minority, consisting of one-sixteenth of these classes, produces little less than two-thirds of it.

BOOK IV

THE REASONABLE HOPES OF LABOUR — THEIR MAGNITUDE, AND THEIR BASIS.

CHAPTER I

How the Future and Hopes of the Labouring Classes are bound up with the Prosperity of the Classes who exercise Ability.

THE conclusion just arrived at is not yet com- pletely stated; for there are certain further facts to be considered in connection with it which have indeed already come under our view, but which, in order to simplify the course of our argument, have been put out of sight in the two preceding chapters. I shall return to these facts presently; but it will be well, before doing so, to take the conclusion as it stands in this simple and broad form, and see, by reference to those principles which were explained at starting, and in which all classes and parties agree, what is the broad lesson which it forces on us, underlying all party differences.

I started with pointing out that, so far

_{The foregoing conclusions not yet complete; but first let us see the lesson which it teaches us as it stands.}

BOOK IV.
CH. I.

If we sum up all that has been said thus far, it may seem at first sight that it teaches nothing but the negative lesson, that we should let Ability have its own way unchecked.

as politics are concerned, the aim of all classes is to maintain their existing incomes; and that the aim of the most numerous class is not only to maintain, but to increase them. I pointed out further that the income of the individual is necessarily limited by the amount of the income of the nation; and that therefore the increase, or at all events the maintenance, of the existing income of the nation is implied in all hopes of social and economic progress, and forms the foundation on which all such hopes are based. I then examined the causes to which the existing income of the nation is due; and I showed that very nearly two-thirds of it is due to the exertions of a small body of men who contribute thus to the productive powers of the community, not primarily because they possess Capital, but because they possess Ability, of which Capital is merely the instrument; that it is owing to the exercise of Ability only that this larger part of the income has gradually made its appearance during the past hundred years; and that were the exercise of Ability interfered with, the increment would at once dwindle, and before long disappear.

Thus the two chief factors in the production of the national income — in the production of that wealth which must be produced before it can be distributed—are not Labour and Capital, which terms, as commonly used, mean living labourers on the one hand, and dead material on the other; but they are two distinct bodies of living men—labourers on the one hand, and on the other men of Ability. The great practical truth, then, which is to be drawn from the foregoing arguments is this—and it is to be drawn from them in the interest of all classes alike—that the action of Ability should never be checked or hampered in such a way as to diminish its productive efficacy, either by so interfering with its control of Capital, or by so diminishing its rewards, as to diminish the vigour with which it exerts itself; but that, on the contrary, all these social conditions should be jealously maintained and guarded which tend to stimulate it most, by the nature of the rewards they offer it, and which secure for it also the most favourable conditions for its exercise. By such means, and by such means only, is there any possibility of the national

BOOK IV.
CH. I.

But this is very far from being the whole lesson taught, or indeed the chief part of it.

wealth being increased, or even preserved from disastrous and rapid diminution.

This, however, is but one half of the case; and, taken by itself, it may seem to have no connection with the problem which forms the main subject of this volume, namely, the social hopes and interests, not of Ability, but of Labour. For, taken by itself, the conclusion which has just been stated may strike the reader at first sight as amounting merely to this: that the sum total of the national income will be largest when the most numerous minority of able men produce the largest possible incomes,—incomes which they themselves consume; and that, unless they are allowed to consume them, they will soon cease to produce them. From the labourer's point of view, such a conclusion would indeed be a barren one. It might show him that he could not better himself by attacking the fortunes of the minority; but it would, on the other hand, fail to show him that he was much interested in their maintenance, since, if Ability consumes the whole of the annual wealth which it adds to the wealth annually produced by Labour, the total might

FROM THE LABOURER'S POINT OF VIEW 241

be diminished by the whole of the added portion, and Labour itself be no worse off than formerly. But when I said just now that it was to the interest of all classes alike not to diminish the rewards which Ability may hope for by exerting itself, this was said with a special qualification. I did not say that it was to the interest of the labourers to allow Ability to retain the whole of what it produced, or to abstain themselves from appropriating a certain portion of it; but what I did say was that any portion appropriated thus should not be so large, nor appropriated in such a way, as to make what remains an object of less desire, or the hope of possessing it less powerful as a stimulus to producing it. This qualification, as the reader will see presently, gives to the conclusion in question a very different meaning from that which at first he may very naturally have attributed to it.

BOOK IV.
CH. I.

For the precise point to which I have been leading up, from the opening page of the present volume to this, is that a considerable portion of the wealth produced by Ability may be taken from it and handed

The chief lesson to be learnt is that, whilst Ability is the chief producer of wealth,

BOOK IV.
CH. I.

Labour may appropriate a large share of its products.

over to Labour, without the vigour of Ability being in the least diminished by the loss; that such being the case, the one great aim of Labour is to constantly take from Ability a certain part of its product; and that this is the sole process by which, so far as money is concerned, Labour has improved its position during the past hundred years, or by which it can ever hope to improve it further in the future.

The question is, How much may it appropriate without paralysing the Ability which produces it?

The practical question, therefore, for the great mass of the population resolves itself into this: What is the extent to which Ability can be mulcted of its products, without diminishing its efficacy as a productive agent? An able man's hopes of securing *nine hundred thousand pounds* for himself would probably stimulate his Ability as much as his hopes of securing a *million*. Indeed the fact that, before he could secure a *million pounds* for himself, he had to produce a *hundred thousand* for other people, might tend to increase his efforts rather than to relax them. But, on the other hand, if, before he could secure a *hundred thousand pounds* for himself, he had to produce a *million* for other people, it is doubtful whether either sum would ever be produced at all. There must therefore be, under any given set of circumstances, some point somewhere between these two extremes up to which Labour can appropriate the products of Ability with permanent advantage to itself, but beyond which it cannot carry the process, without checking the production of what it desires to appropriate. But how are we to ascertain where that precise point is?

To this question it is altogether impossible to give any answer based upon *à priori* reasoning. The very idea of such a thing is ridiculous; and to attempt it could, at the best, result in nothing better than some piece of academic ingenuity, having no practical meaning for man, woman, or child. But what reasoning will not do, industrial history will. Industrial history will provide us with an answer of the most striking kind—general, indeed, in its character; but not, for that reason, any the less decided, or less full of instruction. For industrial history, in a way which few people realise, will show us how, during the past hundred years, Labour

This is a question which can be answered only by experience; and we have the experience of a century to guide us.

has actually succeeded in accomplishing the feat we are considering; how, without checking the development and the power of Ability, it has been able to appropriate year by year a certain share of what Ability produces. When the reader comes to consider this,—which is the great industrial object lesson of modern times,—when he sees what the share is which Labour has appropriated so triumphantly, he will see how the conclusions we have here arrived at, with regard to the causes of production, afford a foundation for the hopes and claims of Labour, as broad and solid as that by which they support the rights of Ability.

Let us turn, then, once more to the fact which I have already so often dwelt upon, that during the closing years of the last century the population of Great Britain was about *ten millions*, and the national income about a *hundred and forty million pounds*. It has been shown that to reach and maintain that rate of production required the exertion of an immense amount of Ability, and the use of an immense Capital which Ability had recently created. But let me repeat what I

THE AMOUNT TAKEN BY LABOUR 245

have said already: that we will, for the purpose of the present argument, attribute the production of the whole to average human Labour. It is obvious that Labour did not produce more, for no more was produced; and it is also obvious that if, since that time, it had never been assisted and never controlled by Ability, the same amount of Labour would produce no more now. We are therefore, let me repeat, plainly understating the case if we say that British Labour by itself—in other words, Labour shut out from, and unassisted by the industrial Ability of the past ninety years — can, at the utmost, produce annually a *hundred and forty million pounds* for every *ten millions* of the population.

And now let us turn from what Labour produces to what the labouring classes[1] have

---

[1] By labouring classes is meant all those families having incomes of less than a *hundred and fifty pounds* a year. The substantial accuracy of this rough classification has already been pointed out. No doubt they include many persons who are not manual labourers; but against this must be set the fact that, according to the latest evidence, there are at least a *hundred and eighty thousand* skilled manual labourers who earn more than a *hundred and fifty pounds*. And, at all events, whether the classes in question are manual labourers or not, they are, with very manifest exceptions, wage-earners

BOOK IV.
CH. 1.

In 1860 Labour took at least twenty-five per cent more than it produced itself, out of the products of Ability; and it now takes about forty-five per cent.

received at different dates within the ninety or hundred years in question. At the time of which we have just been speaking, they received about half of what we assume Labour to have produced. A labouring population of *ten million* people received annually about *seventy million pounds*.[1] Two generations later, the same number of people received in return for their labour about a *hundred and sixty million pounds*.[2] They were twenty-five per cent —that is to say, for whatever money they receive they give work which is estimated at at least the same money value. A schoolmaster, for instance, who receives a *hundred and forty pounds* a year gives in return teaching which is valued at the same sum. School teaching is wealth just as much as a schoolhouse; it figures in all estimates as part of the national income; and therefore the schoolmaster is a producer just as much as the school builder.

[1] This corresponds with Arthur Young's estimate of wages for about the same period.

[2] Statisticians estimate that in 1860 the working classes of the United Kingdom received in wages *four hundred million pounds;* the population then being about twice what it was at the close of the last century. In order to arrive at the receipts of British Labour, the receipts of Irish Labour must be deducted from this total. The latter are proportionately much lower than the former, and could not have reached the sum of *eighty million pounds*. But assuming them to have reached that, and deducting *eighty million pounds* from *four hundred million pounds*, there is left for British Labour *three hundred and twenty million pounds*, to be divided,

OF THE RECEIPTS OF LABOUR

richer than they possibly could have been if, in 1795, they had seized on all the property in the kingdom and divided it amongst themselves. In other words, Labour in 1860, instead of receiving, as it did two generations previously, half of what we assume it to have produced, received twenty-five per cent more than it produced. If we turn from the year 1860 to the present time, we find that the gains of Labour have gone on increasing; and that each *ten millions* of the labouring classes to-day receives in return for its labour *two hundred million pounds*, or over forty per cent more than it produces. And all these calculations are based, the reader must remember, on the ridiculously exaggerated assumption which was made for the sake of argument, that in the days of Watt and Arkwright, Capital, Genius, and Ability had no share in production; and that all the wealth of the country, till the beginning of the present century, was due to the spontaneous efforts of common Labour alone.

And now let us look at the matter from a

roughly speaking, amongst *twenty million* people; which for each *ten millions* yields a *hundred and sixty million pounds*.

BOOK IV.
CH. I.

The gains of Labour are put in a yet more striking light by comparing the present income of Labour with the total income of the country fifty years ago.

point of view slightly different, and compare the receipts of Labour not with what we assume it to have itself produced, but with the total product of the community at a certain very recent date.

In 1843, when Queen Victoria had been six or seven years on the throne, the gross income of the nation was in round numbers *five hundred and fifteen million pounds*. Of this, *two hundred and thirty-five million pounds* went to the labouring classes, and the remainder, *two hundred and eighty million pounds*, to the classes that paid income-tax. Only fifty years have elapsed since that time, and, according to the best authorities, the income of the labouring classes now is certainly not less than *six hundred and sixty million pounds*.[1] That is to say, it exceeds, by a *hundred and forty-five million pounds*, the entire income of the nation fifty years ago.

An allowance, however, must be made for the increase in the number of the labourers. That is of course obvious, and we will at once proceed to make it. But when it is made,

---

[1] According to the latest estimates, it exceeds *seventeen hundred million pounds*.

the case is hardly less wonderful. The labouring classes in 1843 numbered *twenty-six millions*; at the present time they number *thirty-three millions*.[1] That is to say, they have increased by *seven million* persons. Now assuming, as we have done, that Labour by itself produces as much as *fourteen pounds* per head of the population, this addition of *seven million* persons will account for an addition of *ninety-eight million pounds* to the *five hundred and fifteen million pounds* which was the amount of the national income fifty years ago. We must therefore, to make our comparisons accurate, deduct *ninety-eight million pounds* from the *hundred and forty-five million pounds* just mentioned, which will leave us an addition of *forty-seven million pounds*. We may now say, without any reservation, that the labouring classes of this country, in proportion to their number, receive to-day *forty-seven million pounds* a year more

[1] The entire population has risen from about *twenty-seven million five hundred thousand* to *thirty-eight millions*. But a large part of this increase has taken place amongst the classes who pay income-tax, and are expressly excluded from the above calculations. These classes have risen from *one million five hundred thousand* to *five millions*.

BOOK IV.
CH. I.

Every labourer anxious for his own welfare should reflect on these facts.

than the entire income of the country at the beginning of the reign of Queen Victoria.

To any labourer anxious for his own welfare, to any voter or politician of any kind, who realises that the welfare of the labourers is the production of national stability, and who seeks to discover by what conditions that welfare can be best secured and promoted, this fact which I have just stated is one that cannot be considered too closely, too seriously, or too constantly.

Let the reader reflect on what it means.

Dreams of some possible social revolution, dreams of some division of property by which most of the riches of the rich should be abstracted from them and divided amongst the poor—these were not wanting fifty years ago.

They show him that the existing system has done, and is doing for him far more than any Socialist ever promised.

But even the most sanguine of the dreamers hardly ventured to hope that the then riches of the rich could be taken away from them completely; that a sum equal to the rent of the whole landed aristocracy, all the interest on Capital, all the profits of our commerce and manufactures, could be added to what was then the income of the labouring classes. No forces of revolution were thought equal to such a change as that. But what have the facts been? What has happened really? Within fifty years the miracle has taken place, or, indeed, one greater than that. The same number of labourers and their families as then formed the whole labouring population of the country now possess among them every penny of the amount that then formed the income of the entire nation. They have gained every penny that they possibly could have gained if every rich man of that period—if duke, and cotton lord, and railway king, followed by all the host of minor plutocrats, had been forced to cast all they had into the treasury of Labour, and give their very last farthing to swell the labourer's wages. The labourers have gained this; but that is not all. They have gained an annual sum of *forty-seven million pounds* more. And they have done all this, not only without revolution, but without any attack on the fundamental principles of property. On the contrary, the circumstances which have enabled Labour to gain most from the proceeds of Ability, have been the circumstances which have enabled Ability to produce most itself.

BOOK IV.
CH. I.

But before proceeding with this argument, there are two side points to dispose of.

Before, however, we pursue these considerations further, it is necessary that we should deal with two important points which have perhaps already suggested themselves to the reader as essential to the problem before us. They are not new points. They have been discussed in previous chapters; but the time has now arrived to turn to them once again.

CHAPTER II

Of the Ownership of Capital, as distinct from its Employment by Ability.

THE first of the points I have alluded to can be disposed of very quickly. It relates to Land. In analysing the causes to which our national income is due, I began with showing that Land produced a certain definite part of it. For the sake, however, of simplicity, in the calculation which I went on to make, I ignored Land, and the fact of its being a productive agent; and treated the whole income as if produced by Labour, Capital, and Ability. I wish, therefore, now to point out to the reader that this procedure has had little practical effect on the calculation in question, and that any error introduced by it can be easily rectified in a moment. The entire landed rental of this country is, as I have

In the foregoing argument, all mention of Land has been omitted, for simplicity's sake.

Book IV. Ch. II.

But rent, especially the rent of the large owners, is so small a part of the national income that the omission is of no practical importance.

already shown, not so much as one thirteenth of the income; whilst that of the larger landed proprietors is not so much as one thirty-ninth. Now my sole object in dealing with the national income at all is to show how far it is susceptible of redistribution; and it is perfectly certain that no existing political party would attempt, or even desire, to redistribute the rents of any class except the large proprietors only. The smaller proprietors,—*nine hundred and fifty thousand* in number,—who take between them two-thirds of the rental, are in little immediate danger of having their rights attacked. The only rental therefore—namely, that of the larger proprietors—which can be looked on, even in theory, as the subject of redistribution, is too insignificant, being less than *thirty million pounds*, to appreciably affect our calculations when we are dealing with *thirteen hundred millions*. The theory of Land as an independent productive agent, and of rent as representing its independent product, is essential to an understanding of the theory of production generally; but in this country the actual product of the Land is so small, as compared with the products of Labour, Capital, and Ability, that for purposes like the present it is hardly worth considering. Its being redistributed, or not redistributed, would, as we have seen already, make to each individual but a difference of three farthings a day.

The second point I alluded to must be considered at greater length. In dealing with Capital and Ability, I first treated them separately. I then showed that, regarded as a productive agent, Capital *is* Ability, and must be treated as identical with it. But it is necessary, now that we are dealing with distribution, to disunite them for a moment, and treat them separately once more. For even though it be admitted that Ability, working by means of Capital, produces, as it has been shown to do, nearly two-thirds of the national income, and though it be admitted further that a large portion of this product should go to those able men who are actively engaged in producing it,—the men whose Ability animates and vivifies Capital,—it may yet be urged that a portion of it which is very large indeed goes, as a

BOOK IV.
CH. II.

Capital, as distinct from the Ability that uses it, has been omitted also.

We must now again consider it in connection with the classes which never themselves employ it, but live on the interest of it.

fact, to men who do not exert themselves at all, or who, at any rate, do not exert themselves in the production of wealth. These men, it will be said, live not on the products of Ability, but on the interest of Capital which they have come accidentally to possess; and it will be asked on what grounds Labour is interested in forbearing to touch the possessions of those who produce nothing? If it has added to its income, as it has done, during the past hundred years, why should it not now add to it much more rapidly, by appropriating what goes to this wholly non-productive class?

What place do these classes hold in the productive system?

To this question there are several answers. One is that a leisured class—a class whose exertions have no commercial value, or no value commensurate with the cost of its maintenance—is essential to the development of culture, of knowledge, of art, and of mental civilisation generally. But this is an answer which we need not dwell on here; for, whatever its force, it is foreign to our present purpose. We will confine ourselves solely to the material interests that are involved, and consider solely how the plunder of a class

THE HOPE OF INTEREST AS A MOTIVE 257

living on the interest of Capital would tend to affect the actual production of wealth.

It would affect the production of wealth in just the same way as would a similar treatment of that class on whose active Ability production is directly dependent; and it would do this for the following reasons.

The greater part of the Capital that has been accumulated in the modern world is the creation of active Ability, as I have pointed out already. It has been saved not from the product of Labour, but from the product which Ability has added to this. It is Ability congealed, or Ability stored up. And the main motive that has prompted the men of Ability to create it has not consisted only of the desire of enjoying the income which they are enabled to produce by its means, when actually employing it themselves; but the desire also of enjoying some portion of the income which will be produced by its means if it is employed by the Ability of others. In a word, the men who create and add to our Capital are motived to do so by expectation that the Capital shall

BOOK IV.
CH. II.

They are the heirs of Ability, and represent, by their possession of Capital, the main object with which that Capital was originally created.

BOOK IV.
CH. II.

For Capital is created and saved in order that it may yield interest, firstly, to the man who himself created and saved it;

be their own property; that it shall, when they wish it, yield them a certain income independent of any further exertions of their own. Were this expectation rendered impossible, were Capital by any means prevented from yielding interest either to the persons who made and saved it, or those to whom the makers might bequeath it, the principal motive for making or saving it would be gone. If a man, for instance, makes *one thousand pounds* he can, as matters stand, do three things with it, any one of which will gratify him. He can spend it as income, and enjoy the whole of it in that way; he can use it himself as Capital, and so enjoy the profits; or he can let others use it as Capital, and so enjoy the interest. But if he were by any means precluded from receiving interest for it, and desired for any reason to retire from active business, he could do with his *thousand pounds* one of two things only— he could spend it as income, in which case it would be destroyed; or let others use it as Capital, in which case he himself could derive no benefit whatever from it, and would, in effect, be giving it or throwing it away. Were the first course pursued, no Capital would be saved; were the second course obligatory, no Capital would be created.[1]

[1] These considerations are so obvious, and have been so constantly dwelt upon by all economic writers, other than avowed Socialists, that it is quite unnecessary here to insist on these further. Even the Socialists themselves have recognised how much force there is in them, and have consequently been at pains to meet them by the following curious doctrine. They maintain that a man who makes or inherits a certain sum has a perfect right to possess it, to hoard it, or squander it on himself; but no right to any payment for the use made of it by others. They argue that if he puts it into a business he is simply having it preserved for him; for the larger part of the Capital at any time existing would dwindle and disappear if it were not renewed by being used. Let him put it into a business, say the Socialists, and draw it out as he wants it. Few things can show more clearly than this suggested arrangement the visionary character of the Socialistic mind; for it needs but little thought to show that such an arrangement would defeat its own objects and be altogether impracticable. The sole ground on which the Socialists recommend it, in preference to the arrangement which prevails at present, is that the interest which the owners of the Capital are forbidden to receive themselves would by some means or other be taken by the State instead and distributed amongst the labourers as an addition to their wages, and would thus be the means of supplying them with extra comforts. Now the interest if so applied would, it is needless to say, be not saved but consumed. But the owners of the Capital, who are thus deprived of their interest, are to have the privilege, according to the arrangement we are considering, of consuming their Capital in lieu of the interest that has been taken from them. Accordingly, whereas the interest is all that is consumed now, under this arrangement

BOOK IV. CH. II.

And secondly, to his family and his immediate heirs.

The bulk of the Capital owned now by those who do not employ it themselves has come to them from their fathers or grandfathers who created it;

I have spoken thus far as though in creating Capital a man's motive were the hope of enjoying the interest of it himself. But there is another motive almost equally powerful—in some cases more powerful—and that is the hope of transferring or transmitting it to his family or to his children. Now four-fifths of the Capital of the United Kingdom has been created within the last eighty years. The total Capital in 1812 amounted to about *two thousand millions;* now it amounts to almost *ten thousand millions.* Therefore *eight hundred thousand millions* of the Capital of this country has been created by the Ability of the parents and of the grandparents of those who now possess it, supplemented by the Ability of many who now possess it themselves. The most rapid increase in it took place between 1840 and 1875. If we regard men of fifty as

the Capital would be consumed as well. The tendency, in fact, of the arrangement would be neither more nor less than this: to increase the consumption of the nation at the expense of its savings, until at last all the savings had disappeared. It would be impracticable also for many other reasons, to discuss which here would simply be waste of time. It is enough to observe that the fact of its having been suggested is only a tribute to the insuperable nature of the difficulty it was designed to meet.

THE BEQUEST OF CAPITAL

representing the present generation of those actively engaged in business, we may say that their grandfathers made *ten thousand millions* of our existing Capital, their parents *four thousand millions*, and themselves *two thousand millions*. It will thus be easily realised how those persons who own Capital which they leave others to employ, and which personally they have had no hand in making, are for the most part relatives or representatives of the very persons who made it, and who made it actuated by the hope that their relations or representatives should succeed to it. All history shows us that one of the most important and unalterable factors in human action is a certain solidarity of interest between men— even selfish men—and those nearly connected with them; and just as parents are, by an almost universal instinct, prompted to rear their children, so are they prompted to bequeath to them—or, at all events, to one of them—the greater part of their possessions. We might as well try to legislate against the instincts of maternity, as against the instinct of bequest. Therefore, that the ownership of much of the Capital of the country should be

BOOK IV.
CH. II.

As the history of the growth of Capital during the present century shows.

A man's desire to leave money to his family is shown by history to be as strong a motive as the desire to enjoy it himself.

separated from the actual employment of it, is a necessary result of the forces by which it was called into existence; and in proportion as such a result was made impossible in the future, the continued operation of these forces would be checked.

Further, it is impossible to prevent interest being both offered and taken for the use of Capital.

But interest depends also on a reason that is yet stronger and more simple than these. The owner of Capital receives interest for the use of it, because it is, in the very nature of things, impossible to prevent its being offered him, and impossible to prevent his taking it. If a man who possesses *one hundred thousand pounds*, by using it as Capital makes *ten thousand pounds* a year, and could, if he had the use of another *one hundred thousand pounds*, add another *ten thousand pounds* to his income, no Government could prevent his making a bargain with a man who happened to possess the sum required, by which the latter, in return for lending him that sum, would obtain a part of the income which the use of it would enable him to produce.

The most practical aspect of the matter, however, yet remains to be considered. I have spoken of interest as of a thing with

AS THE PRICE OF THE USE OF CAPITAL 263

whose nature we are all familiar. But let us pause and ask, What is it? It is merely a part of the product which active Ability is enabled to produce by means of its tool, Capital. It is the part given by the man who uses the tool to the man who owns it. But the tool, or Capital, is, as we have seen already, itself the product of the Ability of some man in the past; so that the payment of interest, whether theoretically just or no, is a question which concerns theoretically two parties only: the possessor of living Ability, and the possessor of the results of past Ability. Thus, whatever view we may happen to take about it, Labour, in so far as theoretical justice goes, has no concern in the matter, one way or the other. For if interest is robbery, it is Ability that is robbed, not Labour.

It is important to take notice of this truth; for a knowledge of what is theoretically just, though it can never control classes so far as to prevent their seizing on whatever they can obtain and keep, exercises none the less a very strong influence on their views as to how much of the wealth of other classes is obtainable, and also on the temper in which, and the

BOOK IV.
CH. II.

And whether interest be just or no, it at all events represents no injustice to Labour.

BOOK IV.
CH. II.

For it will modify, though not extinguish, their desire to appropriate a part of what is paid as interest.

entire procedure by which, they will endeavour to obtain it. For this reason it is impossible to insist too strongly on the fact that, as a matter of theoretical justice, Labour, as such, has no claim whatever on any of the interest paid for the use of Capital; and that if it succeeds in obtaining any part of this interest, it will be obtaining what has been made by others, not what has been made by itself. It is not that such arguments as these will extinguish the desire of Labour to increase its own wages at the expense of interest, if possible; for might—the might that can sustain itself, not the brute force of the moment—will always form in the long run the practical rule of right; but they will disseminate a dispassionate view of what the limits of possibility are, and on what these limits depend.

History shows us that they have been doing this already,

And now let us turn to the facts of industrial history, and see what light they throw on what has just been said. I have pointed out that if Capital is to be made or used at all, it must necessarily, for many reasons, be allowed to yield interest to its owners; but the amount of interest it yields has varied at various times; and, although to abolish it altogether would be impossible, or, if possible, fatal to production, it is capable, under certain circumstances, of being reduced to a minimum, without production being in any degree checked; and every *pound* which the man who employs Capital is thus relieved from paying to the man who owns it constitutes, other things being equal, a fund which may be appropriated by Labour. To say this is to make no barren theoretical statement. The fund in question not only may, under certain circumstances, be appropriated by Labour; but these circumstances are the natural result of our existing industrial system; and the fund, as I will now show, has been appropriated by Labour already, and forms a considerable part of that additional income which Labour, as we have seen, has secured from the income created by Ability.

In days preceding the rise of the modern industrial system, the average rate of interest was as high as ten per cent. As the modern system developed itself, as Ability more and more was diverted from war, and concentrated on commerce and industry, and produced by the use of Capital a larger and more certain to an increasing extent.

<small>BOOK IV.
CH. II.

Interest now forms but a small part of the income of the nation,</small>

product, the price it paid for the use of Capital fell, till by the middle of this century it was not more than five per cent. During the past forty years it has continued to sink still further, and can hardly be said now to average much more than three.

<small>*In spite of appearances to the contrary;*</small>

This fact is sufficiently well known to investors; but there are other facts known equally well which tend to confuse popular thought on the subject, and which accordingly, in a practical work like this, it is very necessary to place in their true light. For, in spite of what has been said of the fall in the rate of interest from ten to six, and to five, and from five to three per cent, it is notorious that companies, when successful, often pay to-day dividends of from ten to twenty per cent, or even more; and founders' shares in companies are constantly much sought after, which are merely shares in such profits as result over and above a return of at least ten per cent on the capital.

<small>*As much of what is vulgarly considered interest is*</small>

But the explanation of this apparent contradiction is simple. Large profits must not be confounded with high interest. Large profits are a mixture of three things, as was pointed out by Mill, though he did not name two of them happily. He said that profits consisted of wages of superintendence, compensation for risk, and interest on Capital. If, instead of wages of superintendence, we say the product of Ability, and instead of compensation for risk, we say the reward of sagacity, which is itself a form of Ability, we shall have an accurate statement of the case. A large amount of the Capital in the kingdom is managed by the men who own it; and when they manage it successfully, the returns are large. Sometimes a man with a Capital of *a hundred thousand pounds* will make as much as *fifteen thousand pounds* a year; but that does not mean that his Capital yields fifteen per cent of interest. Let such a man be left another *hundred thousand pounds*, which he determines not to put into his own business, but invests in some security held to be absolutely safe, and he will find that interest on Capital means not more than three and a half per cent. If he is determined to get a large return on his Capital, and if he does this by investing it in some new and speculative enterprise, this result, unless it be

BOOK IV.
CH. II.

something quite different.

the mere good luck of a gambler, is mainly the result of his own knowledge and judgment, as the following facts clearly enough show.

Between the years 1862 and 1885 there were registered in the United Kingdom about *twenty-five thousand* joint stock companies, with an aggregate Capital of about *two thousand nine hundred million pounds*. Of these companies, by the year 1885, more than *fifteen thousand* had failed, and less than *ten thousand* were still existing. During the following four years the proportion of failures was smaller; but a return published in 1889 shows that of all the companies formed during the past twenty-seven years, considerably more than half had been wound up judicially. Therefore a man who secures a large return on money invested in a business not under his own control, does so by an exercise of sagacity not only beneficial to himself, but in a still higher degree beneficial to the country generally; for he has helped to direct human exertion into a profitable and useful channel, whereas those who are less sagacious do but help it to waste itself.[1]

[1] The part played in national progress by the mere business sagacity of investors, amounts practically to a con-

Of large returns on Capital, then, only a part is interest; the larger part being merely another name for what we have shown to be the actual creation of Ability—either the Ability with which the Capital has been employed in directing Labour, or the Ability with which some new method of directing Labour has been selected. There is accordingly no contradiction in the two statements that Capital may often bring more than fifteen per cent to the original investors; and yet that interest on Capital in the present day is not more than three or three and a half per cent. Here is the explanation of shares rising in value. A man who at the starting of a business takes *a hundred one pound shares* in it, and, when it is well established, gets *twenty pounds* a year as a dividend, will be able to sell his shares for something like *six hundred pounds;* which means that little more than three per cent is the interest which will be received by the purchaser.

Interest, then, or the sum which those who

stant criticism of inventions, discoveries, schemes, and enterprises of all kinds, and the selection of those that are valuable from amongst a mass of what is valueless and chimerical.

BOOK IV. CH. II.

Interest, then, has decreased, and the whole sum thus saved has gone to the labouring classes.

use Capital pay to those who own it, having decreased, as we have seen it has done, with the development of our industrial system, it remains to show the reader where the sum thus saved has gone. It must have gone to one or other of two classes of people: to the men of Ability, or to the labourers. If it had gone to the former,—that is, to the employers of Labour,—their gains now would be greater, in proportion to the Capital employed by them, than they were fifty years ago; but if their gains have not become greater, then the sum in question must obviously have found its way to the labourers. And that such is the case will be made sufficiently evident by the fact that Mr. Giffen has demonstrated in the most conclusive way that, if rent and the interest taken by the classes that pay income-tax had increased as fast as the sum actually taken by Labour, the sum assessed to income-tax would be *four hundred million pounds* greater than it is, and the sum taken by Labour *four hundred million pounds* less.[1]

---

[1] See Mr. Giffen's Inaugural Address of the Fiftieth Session of the Statistical Society.

In this case the wealthier classes would be now taking *one thousand and sixty million pounds*, instead of the *six hundred million pounds* which they actually do take;[1] and the labouring classes, instead of taking, as they do, *six hundred and sixty million pounds*, or, as Mr. Giffen maintains, more, would be taking only *two hundred and sixty million pounds*.[2] In fact, as Mr. Giffen declares, " It would not be far short of the mark to say that the whole of the great improvement of the last fifty years has gone to the masses." And the accuracy of this statement is demonstrated in a very striking way by the fact that had the whole improvement, according to the contrary hypothesis, gone

[1] The gross amount assessed to income-tax in 1891 was nearly *seven hundred million pounds;* now more than *a hundred million pounds* was exempt, as belonging to persons with incomes of less than *a hundred and fifty pounds* a year. Mr. Giffen maintains (see his evidence given before the Royal Commission on Labour, 7th December 1892) that there is an immense middle-class income not included amongst the wages of the labouring class. This, according to the classification adopted above, which divides the population into those with incomes above, and those with incomes below *a hundred and fifty pounds*, would raise the collective incomes of the latter to over *seven hundred million pounds.*

[2] See Mr. Giffen's Address, as above.

not to the labourers, but to the classes that pay income-tax, the remainder, namely, *two hundred and sixty million pounds*, would correspond, almost exactly, allowing for the increase of their numbers, with what the labouring classes received at the close of the last century.

<small>What the social reformer should study is not the dreams of Socialists, but the forces actually at work, through which Labour has already gained, and is gaining so much.</small>

What, then, the social reformer, what the labourer, and the friend of Labour, ought to study with a view to improving the condition of the labouring classes, is not the theories and dreams of those who imagine that the improvement is to be made only by some reorganisation of society, but the progress, and the causes of the progress, that these classes have actually been making, not only under existing institutions, but through them, because of them, by means of them.

CHAPTER III

Of the Causes owing to which, and the Means by which Labour participates in the growing Products of Ability.

LET me repeat in other words what I have just said. The labouring classes, under the existing condition of things, have acquired more wealth in a given time than the most sanguine Socialist of fifty years ago could have promised them; and this increased wealth has found its way into their pockets owing to causes that are in actual operation round us. These causes, therefore, should be studied for two reasons: firstly, in order that we may avoid hindering their operation; secondly, in order that we may, if possible, accelerate it; and I shall presently point out, as briefly, but as clearly as I can, what the general character of these causes is.

BOOK IV. CH. III.

It is true that there are notorious facts that may make the superficial or excitable observer doubt the reality of this great progress of the labouring classes.

But before doing this,—before considering the cause of this progress,—I must for a moment longer dwell and insist upon the reality of it; because unhappily there are certain notorious facts which constantly obtrude themselves on the observation of everybody, and which tend to make many people deny, or at least doubt it. These facts are as follows.

Speaking in round numbers, there exists in this country to-day a population consisting of about *seven hundred thousand* families, or *three million* persons, whose means of subsistence are either insufficient, or barely sufficient, or precarious, and the conditions of whose life generally are either hard or degrading, or both. A considerable portion of them may, without any sentimental exaggeration, be called miserable; and all of them may be called more or less unfortunate. There is, further, this observation to be made. People who are in want of the bare necessaries of life can hardly be worse off absolutely at one period than another; but if, whilst their own poverty remains the same, the riches of other classes increase, they do, in a certain sense, become worse off relatively. The common statement, therefore, that the

poor are getting constantly poorer is, in this
relative sense, true of a certain part of the
population; and that part is now nearly equal
in numbers to the entire population of the
country at the time of the Norman Conquest.
Such being the case, it is of course obvious
that persons who, for purposes of either bene-
volence or agitation, are concerned to discover
want, misfortune, and misery, find it easier
to do so now than at any former period.
London alone possesses an unfortunate class
which is probably as large as the whole
population of Glasgow; and an endless pro-
cession of rags and tatters might be marched
into Hyde Park to demonstrate every Sunday.
But if the unfortunate class in London is as
large as the whole population of Glasgow, we
must not forget that the population of London
is greater by nearly a *million* than the population of all Scotland; and the truth is that, But when
although the unfortunate class has, with the —viz. facts
increase of population, increased in numbers the very
absolutely, yet relatively, for at least two reduced to
centuries, it has continued steadily to decrease. propor-
In illustration of this fact, it may be mentioned tions,
that, whereas in 1850 there were *nine* paupers

to every *two hundred* inhabitants, in 1882 there were only *five;* whilst, to turn for a moment to a remoter period, so as to compare the new industrial system with the old, in the year 1615, a survey of Sheffield, already a manufacturing centre, showed that the "begging poor," who "could not live without the charity of their neighbours," actually amounted to one-third of the population, or *seven hundred and twenty-five* households out of *two thousand two hundred and seven.* Further, although, as I observed just now, it is in a certain sense true to say that, relatively to other classes, the unfortunate class has been getting poorer, the real tendency of events is expressed in a much truer way by saying that all other classes have been getting more and more removed from poverty.

We shall find that they have no such significance, nor disprove in any way the extraordinary progress of the vast majority.

What the presence, then, and the persistence of this class really shows us is not that the progress of the labouring classes as a whole has been less rapid and less remarkable than it has just been said to be, but that a certain fraction of the population, for some reason or other, has always remained hitherto outside this general progress; and the one practical

TWO CAUSES OF POPULAR PROGRESS 277

lesson which its existence ought to force on us is not to doubt the main movement, still less to interfere with it, but to find some means of drawing these outsiders into it. This great and grave problem, however, requires to be treated by itself, and does not come within the scope of the present volume. Our business is not with the causes which have shut out one-tenth of the poorer classes from the growing national wealth, but with those which have so signally operated in making nine-tenths of them sharers in it.

BOOK IV. CH. III.

What then are the causes of this progress?

We will accordingly return to these, and consider what they are. We shall find them to be of two kinds: firstly, those which consist of the natural actions of men, each pursuing his own individual interest; and secondly, their concerted actions, which represent some general principle, and are deliberately undertaken for the advantage not of an individual but of a class. We will begin with considering the former; as not only are they the most important, but they also altogether determine and condition the latter, and the latter, indeed, can do little more than assist them.

They are of two kinds: spontaneous tendencies, and the deliberate and concerted actions of men.

BOOK IV.
CH. III.

We will begin with the spontaneous tendencies—*i.e.* the natural actions of individuals, each pursuing his own interest.

There are two ways of getting rich: (1) by abstracting from an existing income, or (2) by adding to it. The rich class of the modern world have, as a whole, become rich in the second way.

The natural causes that tend to distribute amongst Labour a large portion of the wealth produced by Ability will be best understood if we first consider for a moment the two ways—and the two only ways—in which a minority can become wealthy. What these are can be easily realised thus. Let us imagine a community of eight labouring men, who make each of them *fifty pounds* a year, and who represent Labour; and let us imagine a ninth man,—a man of Ability,—who represents the minority. The ninth man might, if he were strong enough, rob each of the eight men of *twenty-five pounds*, compelling them each to live on *twenty-five pounds* instead of on *fifty pounds*, and appropriate to himself an annual *two hundred pounds*. Or he might reach the same result in a totally different way. He might so direct and assist the Labour of the eight men, that without any extra effort to themselves they each, instead of *fifty pounds* produced *seventy-five pounds*, and if, under these circumstances, he took *twenty-five pounds* from each, he would gain the same sum as before, namely *two hundred pounds*, but, as I said, in a totally different way. It would represent what he had added to the original product of the labourers, instead of representing anything he had taken from it. Now whatever may have been true of rich classes in former times and under other social conditions, the riches now enjoyed by the rich class in this country have, with exceptions which are utterly unimportant, been acquired by the latter of these two methods, not by the former. They represent an addition to the product of Labour, not an abstraction from it. This is, of course, clear from what has been said already; but it is necessary here to specially bear it in mind.

Let us then take a community of eight labourers, each producing commodities worth *fifty pounds* a year, and each consuming—as he easily might—the whole of them. These men represent the productive power of Labour; and now let us suppose the advent of Ability in the person of the ninth man, by whose assistance this productive power is multiplied, and consider more particularly what the ninth man does. There is one thing which it is quite plain he does not do. He does not multiply the power of Labour for the sake of merely increasing the output of those actual

Let us consider the nature of the process, By first representing Labour and Ability in their simplest imaginable forms; Ability, or the employing class, being represented as one man.

products which he finds the labourers originally producing and consuming, and of appropriating the added quantity; for the things he would thus acquire would be of no possible good to him. He would have more boots and trousers than he could wear, more bread and cheese than he could eat, and spades and implements which he did not want to use. He would not want them himself, and the labourers are already supplied with them. They would be no good to anybody. He does not therefore employ his Ability thus, so as to increase the output of the products that have been produced hitherto; but he enables first, we will say, four men, then three, then two, and lastly one, to produce the same products that were originally produced by eight; and he thus liberates a continually increasing number, whom he sets to produce products of new and quite different kinds.

Let us see how he does this. The eight labourers, when he finds them, make each *fifty pounds* a year, or *four hundred pounds* in the aggregate; and this represents the normal necessaries of their existence. He, by the assistance which his Ability renders Labour, enables at last, after many stages of progress, these same necessaries to be produced by one single man, who, instead of producing, as formerly, goods worth *fifty pounds*, finds himself, with the assistance of Ability, producing goods worth *four hundred pounds*. There is thus an increase of *three hundred and fifty pounds*, and this increment the man of Ability takes.

Meanwhile, seven men are left idle, and with them the man of Ability makes the following bargain. Out of the *three hundred and fifty pounds* worth of necessaries which he possesses, he offers each of them *fifty pounds* worth—the amount which originally they each made for themselves, on condition that they will make other things for him, or put their time at his disposal. They accordingly make luxuries for him, or become his personal servants. For the *three hundred and fifty pounds* he pays them in the shape of necessaries, they return him another *three hundred and fifty pounds* in the shape of commodities or of service; and this new wealth constitutes the able man's income.

Such, reduced to its simplest elements, is the process on which the riches of the rich in the modern world depend. It will be seen,

BOOK IV.
CH. III.

In this case, there being no competition of employers, there would be no natural distribution of the increasing products amongst the labourers.

however, that in the case we have just supposed, the labourers, by the process in question, gain absolutely nothing. Each of them originally made *fifty pounds* a year. He now receives the same sum in wages. But the total product has increased by *three hundred and fifty pounds*, and of this the labourers acquire no share whatever. Nor, supposing them to be inexperienced in the art of combination, is there any means by which they could ever do so. And if our imaginary community were a complete representation of reality, the same would be the case with the labourers in real life.

But let us introduce a second man of Ability competing with the first, and the process of distribution of the increased product amongst the labourers begins at once.

But it must now be pointed out that in one important respect, as a representation of reality, our community is incomplete. It represents the main process by which the riches of the rich are produced; but it offers no parallel to one factor in the real situation, owing to which the labourers inevitably acquire a share in them. In that community the rich classes are represented by a single person, who has no conflicting interests analogous to his own to contend against. But in actual life, so far as this point is concerned, the condition of the rich is different altogether. As looked at from without, they are, indeed, a single body, which may with accuracy be represented as one man; but as looked at from within, they are a multitude of different bodies, whose interests, within certain limits, are diametrically opposed to each other. In order, therefore, to make our illustration complete, instead of one man of Ability we must imagine two. The first, whose fortunes we have just followed, and whom, for the sake of distinctness, we will christen John, has already brought production to the state that has been just described. He has managed to get seven men out of eight to produce luxuries for himself,—luxuries, we will say, such as wine, cigars, and butter,—paying these seven men with the surplus necessaries which, with his assistance, are produced by the eighth man. But of these luxuries the seven men keep none; nor can they give any of them to the eighth man, their fellow. John takes all. But now let us suppose that a second man of Ability, whom we will christen James, appears upon the scene, just as anxious as John to direct Labour by his Ability, and just as capable of making Labour productive. But all the labourers are at present in the pay of John. James therefore must set himself to detach them from John's service; and he accordingly engages that if they will work for him they shall not only each receive the necessaries that John gives them, but a share of the other things that they produce—of the butter, of the cigars, and of the wine—as well. The moment this occurs, John has to make a similar offer; and thus the wages of Labour at once begin to rise. When they have been forced up to a certain point, James and John cease to bid against one another, and each employs a certain number of labourers, till one or other of them makes some new discovery which enables the same amount of some commodity —we will say cigars—as has hitherto been produced by two men, to be produced by one; and thus a new labourer is set free, and is available for some new employment. We must assume that James and John could both employ this man profitably—that is, that they could set him to produce some new object of desire—let us say strawberries; and, this being so, there is again a competition for his labour. He is offered by both employers as much as he has received hitherto, and as the other labourers receive; and he is offered besides a certain number of strawberries. Whichever employer ultimately secures his services, the man has secured some further addition to his income. He has some share in the increasing wealth of the community; and, as John and James continue to compete in increasing the production of all other commodities, some share of each increase will in time go to all the labourers.

One thing only could interfere with this process; and that has been excluded from our supposed community: namely, an increase in its numbers. And a mere increase in the numbers would in itself not be enough. It must be an increase which outstrips the discovery of new ways in which labour may be employed profitably. Let us suppose that to our original eight labourers, eight new labourers are added, who if left to themselves could do just what the first eight could do, namely, produce annual subsistence for themselves to the value of *fifty pounds* each. If, under the management of James or John, the productivity of these men could be multiplied eight-fold, as was the case with the first eight, James and

John would be soon competing for their services, and the second eight, like the first eight, would share in the increased product. But if, owing to all the best land being occupied, and few improvements having been discovered in the methods of any new industries, the productivity of the new men could be increased not eightfold, but only by one-eighth—that is to say, if what each man produces by his unaided Labour could be raised by Ability from *fifty pounds*, not to *four hundred pounds*, but to no more than *fifty-six pounds ten shillings*,—*fifty-six pounds ten shillings* would be the utmost these men would get, even if the Ability of James or John got no remuneration whatever. Meanwhile, however, the first set of workmen are, as we have seen, receiving much more than this. They are receiving each, we will say, *one hundred pounds*. The second set, therefore, naturally envy them their situations, and endeavour to secure these for themselves by offering their Labour at a considerably lower price. They offer it at *ninety pounds*, at *seventy pounds*, or even at *sixty pounds;* for they would be bettering their present situation by accepting even this last sum. This being the case, the original eight labourers have necessarily to offer their Labour at reduced terms also; and thus the wages of Labour are diminished all round.

Such is the inevitable result under such circumstances, if each man — employer and employed alike — follows his own interest at the bidding of common sense. One man is not more selfish than another; indeed, in a bad sense, nobody is selfish at all; and for the result nobody is to blame. The average wages of Labour are diminished for this simple reason, and for no other—that the average product is diminished which each labourer assists in producing. The community is richer absolutely; but it is poorer in proportion to its numbers.[1] Let us see how this works out. The original product of the first eight labourers was *fifty pounds* a head, or *four hundred pounds* in the aggregate. This was raised by the co-operation of Ability to *four hundred pounds* a head, or *three thousand two hundred*

---

[1] If the number of employers does not increase, it is true that they, unlike the employed, will be richer in proportion to their numbers; but they will be poorer in proportion to the number of men employed by them.

pounds in the aggregate. But the second set of labourers, whatever Ability may do for them, cannot be made to produce more than *fifty-six pounds ten shillings* a head, or an aggregate of *four hundred and twenty-five pounds*; and thus, whereas eight labourers produced *three thousand two hundred pounds*, sixteen labourers produce only *three thousand six hundred and fifty-two pounds*, and the average product is lowered from *four hundred pounds* to *two hundred and twenty-eight pounds*.[1]

[1] Thus the old theory of the wage-fund, which has so often been attacked of late, has after all this great residuary truth, namely, that the amount of wealth that is spent and taken in wages is limited by the total amount of wealth produced *in proportion to the number* of labourers who assist in its production. That theory, however, as commonly understood, is no doubt erroneous, though not for the reasons commonly advanced by its critics. The theory of a wage-fund as commonly understood means this—that if there were eight labourers and a capital of *four hundred pounds*, which would be spent in wages and replaced within a year, and if this were distributed in equal shares of *fifty pounds*, it would be impossible to increase the share of one labourer without diminishing that of the others; or to employ more labourers without doing the same thing. But the truth is that if means were discovered by which the productivity of any one labourer could be doubled during the first six months, the whole *fifty pounds* destined for his whole year's subsistence

Wages naturally decline then, owing to an increase of population, when relatively to the population wealth declines also; but only then. On the other hand,—and this is the important point to consider,—so long as a country, under the existing system of production, continues, like our own, to grow richer in proportion to the number of labourers, of every fresh increase in riches the labourers will obtain a share, without any political action or corporate struggle on their part, merely by means of a natural and spontaneous process. And we have now seen in a broad and general way what the character of this process is. It may seem, however, to many people that a study of it and of its results can teach no lesson but the lesson of *laisser faire*, which practically means that the labourers have no interest in politics

This natural power, however, can be regulated by deliberate action, political and other, and made more beneficial to the labourers;

might be paid to him during the first six months, and the fund would meanwhile have been created with which to pay him a similar sum for the next six months—the employer gaining in the same proportion as the labourer. So, too, with regard to an additional number of labourers—if ability could employ their labour to sufficient advantage, part of the sum destined to support the original labourer for the second six months of the year might be advanced to them, and before the second six months' wages became due there might be enough to pay an increased wage to all.

at all, and that all social legislation and corporate action of their own is no better than a waste of trouble, and is very possibly worse. But to think this is to completely misconceive the matter. Even a study of this process of natural distribution by itself would be fruitful of suggestions of a highly practical kind; but if we would understand the actual forces to which distribution is due, it must, as I have said already, not be studied by itself, but taken in connection with others by which its operation has been accelerated. I spoke of these as consisting of deliberate and concerted actions in contradistinction to individual and spontaneous actions; and these, speaking broadly, have been of two kinds—the one represented by the organisation of Labour in Trade Unions, the other by certain legislative measures, which, in a vague and misleading way, are popularly described as "Socialistic." Let us proceed to consider these.

Which action takes two chief forms—legislation, and combinations amongst the labourers. We will discuss both in the next chapter.

CHAPTER IV

Of Socialism and Trade Unionism—the Extent and Limitation of their Power in increasing the Income of Labour.

I WILL speak first of the kind of legislation, popularly called Socialistic, which certain people now regard with so much hope, and others with corresponding dread; and I shall show that both of these extreme views rest on a complete misconception of what this so-called Socialism is. For what is popularly called Socialism in this country, so far as it has ever been advocated by any political party, or has been embodied in any measure passed or even proposed in Parliament, does not embody what is really the distinctive principle of Socialism. Socialism, regarded as a reasoned body of doctrine, rests altogether on a peculiar theory of production, to which

<small>Legislation of the kind just alluded to is commonly called Socialistic:</small>

<small>But this way of describing it is inaccurate;</small>

already I have made frequent reference—a theory according to which the faculties of men are so equal that one man produces as much wealth as another; or, if any man produces more, he is so entirely indifferent as to whether he enjoys what he produces or no, that he would go on producing it just the same, if he knew that the larger part would at once be taken away from him. Hence Socialists argue that the existing rewards of Ability are altogether superfluous, and that the existing system of production, which rests on their supposed necessity, can be completely revolutionised and made equally efficacious without them.

But whatever may be the opinions of a few dreamers or theorists, or however in the future these opinions may spread, the fundamental principle of Socialism, up to the present time, has never been embodied in any measure or proposal which has been advocated in this country by any practical party. On the contrary, the proposals and measures which are most frequently denounced as Socialistic—even one so extreme as that of free meals for children at Board Schools

—all presuppose the system of production which is existing, and thus rest on the very foundation which professed Socialists would destroy.[1] They merely represent so many ways—wise or unwise—of distributing a public

Book IV. Ch. IV. As all the so-called Socialistic legislation in this country rests on the very system of production which professed Socialists aim at destroying.

[1] This is true even of productive or distributive industries carried out by the State. The real Socialistic principle of production has never been applied by the State, or by any municipal authority; nor has any practical party so much as suggested that it should be. The manager of a State factory has just the same motive to save that an ordinary employer has: he can invest his money, and get interest on it. A State or a municipal business differs only from a private Capitalist's business either in making no profits, as is the case in the building of ships of war; or of securing the services of Ability at a somewhat cheaper rate, and, in consequence, generally diminishing its efficacy. Of State business carried on at a profit, the Post Office offers the best example; and it is the example universally fixed on by contemporary English Socialists. It is an example, however, which disproves everything that they think it proves; and shows the necessary limitations of the principle involved, instead of the possibility of its extension. For, in the first place, the object aimed at—*i.e.* the delivery of letters—is one of exceptional simplicity. In the second place, all practical men agree that, could the postal service be carried out by private and competing firms, it would (at all events in towns) be carried out much better; only the advantages gained in this special and exceptional case from the entire service being under a single management, outweigh the disadvantages. And lastly, the business, as it stands, is a State business in the most superficial sense only. The railways and the

revenue, which consists almost entirely of taxes on an income produced by the forces of Individualism.

Now, so far as the matter is a mere question of words, we may call such proposals or measures Socialistic if we like. On grounds of etymology we should be perfectly right in doing so; but we shall see that in that case, with exactly the same propriety, we may apply the word to the institution of Government itself. The Army, the Navy, and more obviously still the Police Force, are all Socialistic in this sense of the word; nor can anything be more completely Socialistic than a public road or a street. In each case a certain something is supported by a common fund for the use of all; and every one is entitled to an equal advantage from it, irrespective of

steamers that carry the letters are all the creations of private enterprise, in which the principle of competition, and the motive force of the natural rewards of Ability, have had free play. Indeed the Post Office, as we now know it, if we can call it Socialistic at all, represents only a superficial layer of State Socialism resting on individualism, and only made possible by its developments. Real State Socialism would be merely the Capitalistic system minus the rewards of that Ability by which alone Capital is made productive.

his own deserts, or the amount he has contributed to its support.

If, then, we agree to call those measures Socialistic to which the word is popularly applied at present, Socialism, instead of being opposed to Individualism, is its necessary complement, as we may see at once by considering the necessity of public roads and a police force; for the first of these shows us that private property would be inaccessible without the existence of social property; and the second that it would be insecure without the existence of social servants. The good or evil, then, that will result from Socialism, as understood thus, depends altogether on questions of degree and detail. There is no question as to whether we shall be Socialistic or no. We must be Socialistic; and we always have been, though perhaps without knowing it, as M. Jourdain talked prose. The only question is as to the precise limits to which the Socialistic principle can be pushed with advantage to the greatest number.

What these limits may be it is impossible to discuss here. Any general discussion of such a point would be meaningless. Each

BOOK IV.
CH. IV.

What is called Socialism in this country is a necessary part of every State;

And the principle may probably be extended with good results, if not pushed too far.

case or measure must be discussed on its own merits. But, though it is impossible to state what the limits are, it is exceedingly easy to show on what they depend. They depend on two analogous and all-important facts, one of which I have already explained and dwelt upon, and which forms, indeed, one of the principal themes of this volume. This is the fact, that the most powerful of our productive agents, namely Ability, cannot be robbed, without diminishing its productivity, of more than a certain proportion of the annual wealth produced by it; and, as it is from this wealth that most of the Socialistic fund must be appropriated, Socialistic distribution is limited by the limits of possible appropriation. The other fact — the counterpart of this — is as follows. Just as Ability is paralysed by robbing it of more than a certain portion of its products, Labour may equally be paralysed by an unwise distribution of them; and thus their continued production be at last rendered impossible. For instance, quite apart from any initial difficulty in raising the requisite fund from the wealthier class of tax-payers, the providing of free meals for children in

Board Schools is open to criticism, on account of the effect which it might conceivably have upon parents, of diminishing their industry by diminishing the necessity for its exercise. Whether such would be the effect really in this particular case, it is beside my purpose to consider; but few people will doubt that if such a provision were extended, and if, even for so short a time as a single six months, free meals were provided for the parents also, half the Labour of the country would be for the time annihilated. Labour, however, is as necessary to production as is Ability, even though, under modern conditions, it does not produce so much; and it is therefore perfectly evident that there is a limit somewhere, beyond which to relieve the individual labourer of his responsibilities by paying his expenses out of a public fund will be, until human nature is entirely changed, to dry up the sources from which that fund is derived.

As I have said already, it is impossible, in any general way, to give any indication of what this limit is; but the industrial history of this country supplies a most instructive instance in which it was notoriously over-passed, and what was meant as a benefit to Labour, under circumstances of exceptional difficulty, ended by endangering the prosperity of the whole community. I refer to our Poor Law at the beginning of this century, the effects of which form one of the most remarkable object-lessons by which experience has ever illustrated a special point in economics. That Poor Law, as Professor Marshall well observes, "arranged that part of the wages [of the labourers] should be given in the form of poor relief; and that this should be distributed amongst them in the inverse proportion to their industry, thrift, and forethought. The traditions and instincts," he adds, "which were fostered by that evil experience are even now a great hindrance to the progress of the working classes."[1] Now that particular evil on which Professor Marshall comments,—namely, that the part of the wages coming through this Socialistic channel were in the inverse proportion to what had really been produced by the labourer—is inherent in all

Marginalia: BOOK IV. CH. IV. — The sort of natural limit that there is to its beneficial effects is shown by the history of our Poor Laws.

---

[1] *Principles of Economics*, by Alfred Marshall, book iv. chap. vii.

Socialistic measures, the principal object of which is to raise or supplement wages; as is clearly enough confessed by the Socialistic motto, "To every man according to his needs." It may accordingly be said that, absolutely necessary as the Socialistic principle is, and much as may be hoped from its extension in many directions, it neither has been in the past, nor can possibly be in the future, efficacious to any great extent in increasing the actual income of the labourer.[1]

Such Socialism, whatever good it may do, can never do much in the way of raising money wages.

[1] Though I have aimed at excluding from this volume all controversial matter, I may here hazard the opinion that the Socialistic principle is most properly applied to providing the labourers, not with things that they would buy if they were able to do so, but things that naturally they would not buy. Things procurable by money may be divided into three classes—things that are necessary, things that are superfluous, and things that are beneficial. Clothing is an example of the first class, finery of the second, and education of the third. If a man receives food from the State, otherwise than as a reward for a given amount of labour, his motive to labour will be lessened. If a factory girl, irrespective of her industry, was supplied by the State with fashionable hats and jackets, her motive to labour would be lessened also; for clothing and finery are amongst the special objects to procure which labour is undertaken. But desire to be able to pay for education does not constitute, for most men and women, a strong motive to labour; and therefore education may be supplied by the State, without the efficacy of their labour being interfered with.

BOOK IV. CH. IV.

Trade Unionism in this way can do far more. We will see first how, and then within what limits.

Such being the case, then, let us now turn our attention to another principle of an entirely different kind, which, so far as regards this object, is incalculably more important, and which has constantly operated in the past, and may operate in the future, to increase the labourer's income, without any corresponding disadvantages. I mean that principle of organisation amongst the labourers themselves which is commonly called Trade Unionism; and which directly or indirectly represents the principal means by which Labour is attempting, throughout the civilised world, to accelerate and regulate the natural distribution of wealth. I will first, in the light of the conclusions we have already arrived at, point out to the reader what, speaking generally, is the way in which Trade Unionism strengthens the hands of Labour; and then consider what is the utmost extent to which the strength which Labour now derives from it may be developed.

The operation of Trade Unionism in raising wages can

If the reader has not already forgotten our imaginary community,— our eight labourers with John and James directing them,— our easiest course will be to turn again to that.

We saw that when the labourers were employed by John only,—John who found them each making *fifty pounds* a year, and enabled them by his Ability each to make *four hundred pounds* — we saw that the whole of this increase, in the natural course of things, would be kept by John himself, by whose Ability it was practically created ; for it would not be to John's advantage to part with any of it, and the labourers, so long as they all acted separately, would have no means of extracting any of it from him. It would be useless for one of them at a time to strike for higher wages. The striker and the employer would meet on wholly unequal terms ; because the striker, whilst the strike lasted, would be sacrificing the whole of his income, whilst depriving the employer of only an eighth part of his. But let us alter the supposition. Let us suppose that the labourers combine together, and that the whole eight strike for higher wages simultaneously. The situation is now completely changed ; and the loss that the struggle will entail on both parties is equal. The employer, like the labourer, will for a time lose all his income. It is true

may be easily seen at a glance by reference to the simple community which was imagined in the last chapter.

that if the employer has a reserve fund on which he can support himself whilst production is suspended, and if the labourer has no such fund, the employer may still be sure of an immediate victory, should he be resolved at all costs to resist the labourers' demand. But, in any case, the cost of resisting it will be appreciable: it is a loss which the labourers will be able to inflict on him repeatedly; and he may see that they would be able, by their strikes, to make him ultimately lose more than he would by assenting to their demands, or, at all events, making some concessions to them. It is therefore obvious that the labourers, in such a case, will be able to extract extra wages in the inverse proportion to the loss which the employer will sustain if he concedes them, and in direct proportion to the loss which would threaten him should he refuse to do so.[1]

[1] In our imaginary community we have at first eight labourers, who produce *fifty pounds* a year a-piece = *four hundred pounds*. Then we have eight labourers + one able man, who produce *four hundred pounds* a year for each labourer = *three thousand two hundred pounds*. Of this the able man takes *two thousand eight hundred pounds*. Now, suppose the labourers strike for double wages, and succeed in getting them, their total wages are *eight hundred pounds* a year instead of *four hundred pounds;* and the employer's income

There is, however, much more to be said. With each increase of their wages which the labourers succeed in gaining, they will be better equipping themselves for any fresh struggle in the future; for they will be able to set aside a larger and larger fund on which to support themselves without working, and thus be in a position to make the struggle longer, or, in other words, to inflict still greater injury on the employer. And if such will be

is *two thousand four hundred pounds* instead of *two thousand eight hundred pounds*. The labourers gain a hundred per cent; the employer loses little more than fourteen per cent. The labourers therefore have a stronger motive in demanding than the employer has in resisting. But let us suppose that, the total income of the community remaining unchanged, the labourers have succeeded in obtaining *one thousand eight hundred pounds*, thus leaving the employer *one thousand four hundred pounds*. The situation will now be changed. The labourers could not possibly now gain an increase of a hundred per cent, for the entire income available would not supply this; but let us suppose they strike for an increase of *two hundred pounds*. If they gained that, their income would be *two thousand pounds*, and that of the employer *one thousand two hundred pounds;* but the former situation would be reversed. The employer now would lose more than the labourer would gain. The labourers would gain, in round numbers, only eleven per cent; and the employer would lose fourteen per cent. Therefore the employer would have a stronger motive in resisting than the labourers in demanding.

Combination amongst labourers puts them at an advantage as against competing employers, until their demands grow so unreasonable as to force the employers to combine.

the case when there is one employer only, much more will it be the case when there are two—when John and James, as we have seen, are forced by the necessities of competition to grant part of the labourers' demands, even before they are formulated. It might thus seem that there is hardly any limit to the power which a perfected system of Trade Unionism may one day confer upon the labourers. There are, however, two which we will consider now, in addition to others at which we will glance presently. One is the limit with which we are already familiar, and of which in this connection I shall again speak, namely, the limit of the minimum reward requisite as a stimulus to Ability. The other is a limit closely connected with this, which is constituted by the fact that if the demands of Labour are pushed beyond a certain point against disunited employers, the employers will combine against Labour, as Labour has combined against them, and all further concessions will be, at all costs, unanimously refused.

The ultimate tendency of Trade Unionism

Now a situation like this is the ultimate situation which all Trade Unionism tends to bring about. It tends, by turning the labourers into a single body on the one hand, and the employers into a single body on the other, to make the dispute like one between two individuals; and though for many reasons this result can never be entirely realised,[1] the limits

Marginal note: BOOK IV. CH. IV. is to make any conflict between the employer and employed like a conflict between two individuals.

[1] The possibility of such a result would depend upon two assumptions, which are not in accordance with reality, and for which allowance must be made. The first is the assumption that the labouring population is stationary; the second is that Ability can increase the productivity of Labour equally in all industries. In reality, however, as was noticed in the last chapter, the number of labourers increases constantly, and the improvements in different industries are very unequal; and, owing to these two causes, it often happens that the total value produced in some industries by Labour and Ability together is not so great as is the share that is taken by Labour in others. Thus the labourers employed in the inferior industries could by no possibility raise their wages to the amount received by the labourers employed in the superior ones. Their effort accordingly would be to obtain employment in the latter, and to do so by accepting wages higher indeed than what they receive at present, but lower than those received by the men whose positions they wish to take. Thus, under such circumstances, a union of industrial interests ceases to be any longer possible. By an irresistible and automatic process, there is produced an antagonism between them; and the labourers who enjoy the higher wages will do what is actually done by our Trade Unions: they will form a separate combination to protect their own interests, not only against the employers, but even more directly against other labourers. At a certain stage of their demands, the labourers may be able to combine

BOOK IV.
CH. IV.

of the power of Trade Unionism can be best seen by imagining it. What, then, is the picture we have before us? We have Labour and Ability in the character of two men confronting each other, each determined to secure for himself the largest possible portion of a certain aggregate amount of wealth which they produce together. Now we will assume, though this is far from being the case, that neither of them would shrink, for the sake of gaining their object, from inflicting on the other the utmost injury possible; and we shall see also, if we make our picture accurate, that Labour is physically the bigger man of the two. It happens, however, that the very existence of the wealth for the possession of which they are prepared to fight is entirely dependent on their peacefully co-operating to produce it; so that if in the struggle either disabled the other, he would be destroying the prize which it is the object of his struggle to secure. Thus the dispute between them, however hostile may be

more readily and more closely than the employers; but when a certain stage has been passed, the case will be the reverse. The employers will be forced more and more into unanimous action, whilst the labourers, by their diverging interests, are divided into groups whose action is mutually hostile.

their temper, must necessarily be of the nature not of a fight, but of a bargain; and will be settled, like other bargains, by the process of compromise which Adam Smith calls "the higgling of the market." When such a bargain is struck, there will be a limit on both sides: a maximum limit to what Ability will consent to give, and a minimum limit to what Labour will consent to receive. There will be a certain minimum which Ability must concede in the long run; because if it did not give so much, it would indirectly lose more: and conversely there is a certain maximum more than which Labour will never permanently obtain; because if it did so the stimulus to Ability would be weakened, and the total product would in consequence be diminished, out of which alone the increased share which Labour demands can come.

The limit to which it can raise wages is fixed by the minimum reward that suffices to make Ability operative.

Thus the extent to which Trade Unionism can assist in raising wages, no matter how wide and how complete its development, is far more limited than appearances lead many people to suppose. For the labourers, not only in this country, but all over the world, are growing yearly more expert in the art of effective combination, and are increasing their

Thus the possible power of Trade Unionism in raising wages is far more limited than it seems

strength by a vast network of alliances; and from time to time the whole civilised world is startled at the powers of resistance and destruction which they show themselves to have acquired, and which they have called into operation with a view to enforcing their demands. The gas-strikes and the dock-strikes in London, and the great railway-strikes, and the strike at Homestead in America, are cases in point, and are enough to illustrate my meaning. They impress the imagination with a sense that Labour is becoming omnipotent. But in all these Labour movements there is one unchanging feature, which seems never to be realised either by those who take part in them or by observers, but on which really their entire character depends, and which makes their actual character entirely different from what it seems to be. That this feature should have so completely escaped popular notice is one of the most singular facts in the history of political blindness, and can be accounted for only by the crude and imperfect state in which the analysis of the causes of production has been left hitherto by economists. The feature I allude to is as follows.

These great developments of Trade Unionism which are commonly called Labour movements do not really, in any accurate sense, represent Labour at all. All that they represent in themselves is a power to abstain from labouring. In other words, the increased command of the labourers over the machinery of combination, and even their increased command of the tactics of industrial warfare, represents no increased command over the smallest of industrial processes, nor puts them in a better position, without the aid of Ability, to maintain—still less to increase by the smallest fraction — the production of that wealth in which they are anxious to share farther. A strike therefore, however great or however admirably organised, no more represents any part of the power of Labour than the mutiny organised amongst the crew of Columbus, with a view to making him give up his enterprise, represented the power which achieved the discovery of America. And this is not true of the average labourers only; it is yet more strikingly true of the superior men who lead them. From the ranks of the labourers, men are constantly rising whose

BOOK IV. CH. IV.

The imperfect state of economic science has allowed a totally false idea to be formed as to the force which Trade Unionism represents.

The force which it represents is not Labour at all, but a power of combining in order to abstain from labour.

abilities for organising resistance are remarkable, and indeed admirable; but it is probably not too much to say that no leader who has devoted himself to organising the labourers for resistance has ever been a man capable, to any appreciable degree, of giving them help by rendering their labour more productive. Those who have been most successful in urging their fellows to *ask* for more, have been quite incompetent to help them to *make* more. Thus these so-called Labour leaders, no matter how considerable may be many of their intellectual and moral qualities, are indeed leaders of labourers; but they are no more leaders of Labour than a sergeant who drilled a volunteer corps of art students could be called the leader of a rising school of painting; and a strike is no more the expression of the power of Labour than Byron's swimming across the Hellespont was an expression of the power of poetry, or than Burns's poetry was an expression of the power of ploughing. A strike is merely an expression of the fact that the labourers, for good or ill, can acquire, under certain circumstances, the power to cease from labouring, and can use this as a weapon not of production, but of warfare. The utmost that the power embodied in Trade Unionism could accomplish would be to bring about a strike that was universal; and although no doubt it might do this theoretically, it could never do so much as this practically, for the simple reason that, as I have already pointed out, Labour could not be entirely suspended for even a single day. Further, the more general the suspension was, the shorter would be the time for which it could be maintained; and to mention yet another point to which I have referred already, it could be maintained only, for no matter how short a time, by the assistance of the very thing against which strikes are ostensibly directed, namely Capital; and not even Capital could make that time long. Nature, who is the arch-taskmaster, and who knows no mercy, would soon smash like matchwood a Trade Union of all the world, and force the labourers to go back to their work, even if no such body as an employing class existed.

BOOK IV. CH. IV.

And even this power could never be universal, nor last long; and whilst it lasts it depends on Capital.

All the ideas, then, derived from the recent developments of Trade Unionism, that Labour, through its means, will acquire any greatly increasing power of commanding an increasing share of the total income of the community, rests on a total misconception of the power that Trade Unionism represents, and a total failure to see the conditions and things that limit it. It is limited firstly by Nature, who makes a general strike impossible; secondly by Capital, without which any strike is impossible; and lastly by the fact that the labourers of the present day already draw part of their wages from the wealth produced by Ability; that any further increase they must draw from this source entirely; and that, being thus dependent on the assistance of Ability now, Trade Unionism, as we have seen, has not the slightest tendency to make them any the less dependent on it in the future.

When the reader takes into account all that has just been said, he will be hardly disposed to quarrel with the following conclusions of Professor Marshall, who derives them from history quite as much as from theory, and who expresses himself with regard to Trade Unions thus: "Their importance," he says, "is certainly great, and grows rapidly; but it is apt to be exaggerated: for indeed many of them are little more than eddies such as have always fluttered over the surface of progress. And though they are now on a larger and more imposing scale in this age than before, yet much as ever the main body of the movement depends on the deep, silent, strong stream of the tendencies of Normal Distribution and Exchange."

But in the case of Trade Unionism, just as in that of Socialism, because the extent is limited to which it can raise the labourers' income, it does not follow that within these limits its action may not be of great and increasing benefit. Thus Mill, whose general view of the subject coincides broadly with that of Professor Marshall, points out that though a Union will never be able permanently to raise wages above the point to which in time they would rise naturally, nor permanently to keep them above a point to which they would naturally fall, it can hasten the rise, which might otherwise be long delayed, and retard the fall, which might otherwise be premature; and the gain to Labour may thus in the long run be enormous. Unions have done this for Labour in the past; and with improved and extended organisation, they may be able to do

Trade Unionism, in raising wages, can do little more than accelerate or regulate a rise that would take place owing to other causes.

But none the less it may be of great benefit to the labourers, and remove many evils which a general rise in wages has not removed, and could not remove by itself.

it yet more effectively in the future; and they have done, and may continue to do many other things besides—to do them, and to add to their number. It is beyond my purpose to speak of these things in detail. In the next chapter, I shall briefly indicate some of them; but the main points on which I am concerned to insist are simpler; and the next chapter—the last—will be devoted principally to these.

CHAPTER V

Of the enormous Encouragement to be derived by Labour from a true View of the Situation; and of the Connection between the Interests of the Labourer and Imperial Politics.

THE object of this work, as I explained in the opening chapter, is to point out to the great body of the people—that is to say, to the multitude of average men and women, whose incomes consist of the wages of ordinary Labour—the conditions which determine the possibility of these incomes being increased, and so to enable them to distinguish the true means from the false, which they may themselves adopt with a view to obtaining this result. And in order to show them how their present incomes may be increased, I have devoted myself to showing the reader how their present incomes have been obtained. I

Let me again remind the reader of the object of this book.

It is to show that the labourer's income depends on the general

have done this by fixing his attention on the fact that their present incomes obviously depend upon two sets of causes: first, the forces that produce the aggregate income of the country; and secondly, the forces that distribute a certain portion of this amongst the labourers. And these last I have examined from two points of view; first exhibiting their results, and then indicating their nature. Let me briefly recapitulate what I have said about both subjects.

> BOOK IV.
> CH. V.
>
> forces of production firstly, and secondly on those of distribution.

I have shown that, contrary to the opinion which is too commonly held, and which is sedulously fostered by the ignorance alike of the agitator and the sentimentalist, the forces of distribution which are actually at work around us, which have been at work for the past hundred years, and which are part and parcel of our modern industrial system, have been and are constantly securing for Labour a share of every fresh addition to the total income of the nation; and have, for at all events the past fifty years, made the average income of the labouring man grow faster than the incomes of any other members of the community. They have, in fact, been doing the very thing which the agitator declared

> I have just shown how the normal forces of distribution are all in favour of the labourer, contrary to the vulgar view of the matter.

could be done only by resisting them; and they have not only given Labour all that the agitator has promised it, but they have actually given it more than the wildest agitator ever suggested to it. I have shown the reader this; and I have shown him also that the forces in question are primarily the spontaneous forces—"deep, strong, and silent," as Professor Marshall calls them—"of normal distribution and exchange"; how that these have been, and are seconded by the deliberate action of men: by extended application of what is called the Socialistic principle, and to a far greater extent by combinations of the labourers amongst themselves.

The practical moral of all this is obvious. As to the normal and spontaneous forces of distribution, what a study of them inculcates on the labourer is not any principle of political action, but a general temper of mind towards the whole existing system. It inculcates general acquiescence, instead of general revolt. Now temper of mind, being that from which policies spring, is quite as important as the details of any of the policies themselves. Still it must be admitted that were the normal forces of distribution the only forces that had been at work for the labourer's benefit, the principal lesson they would teach him would be the lesson of *laisser aller*. But though these forces have been the primary, they have not been the only forces; and the deliberate policies by which men have controlled their operation, and have applied them, have been equally necessary in producing the desired results. The normal forces of distribution may be compared to the waters of the Nile, which would indeed, as the river rises, naturally fertilise the whole of the adjacent country, but which would do as much harm as good, and do but half the good they might do, if it were not for the irrigation works devised by human ingenuity. And what these works are to the Nile, deliberate measures have been to the normal forces of distribution. The growing volume of wealth, which is spreading itself over the fields of Labour, even yet has failed to reach an unhappy fraction of the community; the tides and currents flow with intermittent force, which is often destructive, still more often wasted, rarely husbanded and applied to the best advantage. Had it not been for the deliberate action of men,—for legislation in favour of the labourers, and their own combinations amongst themselves, —these evils which have accompanied their general progress would have been greater. Wise action in the future will undoubtedly make them less; and may, though it is idle to hope for Utopias in this world, cause the larger and darker part of them to disappear.

<small>This should encourage, and not discourage, political action on behalf of the labourers.</small>

The lesson, then, to be drawn from what I have urged in the preceding chapter is, taken as a whole, no lesson of *laisser faire*. Though neither Socialism nor Trade Unionism may have much, or perhaps any, efficacy in raising the maximum of the labourer's actual income,—though this must depend on forces which are wholly different,—yet Trade Unionism, and the principle which is called Socialism, may be of incalculable service in bringing about conditions under which that income may be earned with greater certainty, and under improved circumstances, and, above all, be able to command more comforts, conveniences, and enjoyments. Thus many of these measures which I have called Socialistic under protest, may be regarded as an interception of a portion of the labourer's income, and an expenditure of it on his account by the State in a way from which he derives far more benefit than he would, or could have secured if he had had the spending of it himself; whilst Trade Unionism, though it cannot permanently raise his wages beyond a maximum determined by other causes, may, as has been said before, raise them to this earlier than they would have risen otherwise, and prevent what might otherwise occur—a fall in them before it was imperative. Trade Unionism, however, has many other functions besides the raising of wages. It aims — and aims successfully — at diminishing the pain and friction caused amongst the labourers by the vicissitudes alike of industry and of life. It has done much in this direction already; and in the future it may do more.

The fact then that the normal forces of distribution must, if things continue their present course, increase the income of the labourer, even without any action on their own part, though it is calculated to change the temper in which the labourers approach politics, is, instead of being calculated to damp their political activity, calculated to animate it with far more hope and interest than the wild denunciations and theories of the contemporary agitator, which those who applaud them do but half believe. It will to the labourer be far more encouraging to feel that the problem before him is not how to undermine a vast system which is hostile to him, and which, though often attacked, has never yet been subverted, but merely to accommodate more completely to his needs a system which has been, and is, constantly working in his favour.

Let him consider the situation well. Let him realise what that system has already done for him. In spite of the sufferings which, owing to various causes, were inflicted on the labouring classes during the earlier years of the century,—many of them of a kind whose recurrence improved policy may obviate, —the income of Labour has, on the aggregate, continued to rise steadily. Let him consider how much. I have stated this once, let me state it now again. During the first sixty years of this century the income of the

Whilst as to mere wages, if the labourers will judge of the possible near future from the actual near past, the prospects before them must exceed their wildest dreams hitherto.

labouring classes rose to such an extent that in the year 1860 it was equal (all deductions for the increase of population being made) to the income of all classes in the year 1800. But there is another fact, far more extraordinary, to follow; and that is, that a result precisely similar has been accomplished since in one-half of the time. In 1880 the income of the labouring classes was (all deductions for the increase of population being made) more than equal to the income of all classes in the year 1850. Thus the labouring classes in 1860 were in precisely the same pecuniary position as the working classes in 1800 would have been had the entire wealth of the kingdom been in their hands; and the working classes of to-day are in a better pecuniary position than their fathers would have been could they have plundered and divided between them the wealth of every rich and middle-class man at the time of the building of the first Great Exhibition. I repeat what I have said before — that this represents a progress, which the wildest Socialist would never have dreamed of promising.

And now comes what is practically the

important deduction from these facts. What has happened in the near past, will, other things being equal, happen in the near future. If the same forces that have been at work since the year 1850 continue to be at work, and if, although regulated, they are not checked, the labourers of this country will in another thirty years have nearly doubled the income which they enjoy at present. Their income will have risen from something under *seven hundred millions* to something over *thirteen hundred millions*. The labourers, in fact, will, so far as money goes, be in precisely the same position as they would be to-day if, by some unheard-of miracle, the entire present income of the country were suddenly made over to them in the form of wages, and the whole of the richer classes were left starving and penniless. This is no fanciful calculation. It is simply a plain statement of what must happen, and will happen, if only the forces of production continue to operate for another thirty years as they have been operating steadily for the past hundred. Is not this enough to stimulate the labourer's hopes, and convince him that for him the true industrial policy is one that will adjust his own relations with the existing system better, and regulate better the flow of the wealth which it promises to bring him, rather than a policy whose aim is to subvert that system altogether, and in especial to paralyse the force from which it derives its efficacy?

But the one point to remember is that all their prosperity depends on the continued action of Ability, and the best conditions being secured for its operation.

And this brings me back to that main, that fundamental truth which it is the special object of this volume to elucidate. The force which has been at the bottom of all the labourers' progress during the past, and on the continued action of which depends all these hopes for their future—that force is not Labour but Ability; it is a force possessed and exercised not by the many but by the few. The income which Labour receives already is largely in excess of what Labour itself produces. Were Ability crippled, or discouraged from exerting itself, the entire income of the nation would dwindle down to an amount which would not yield Labour so much as it takes now; whilst any advance, no matter how small, on what Labour takes now must come from an increasing product, which Ability only can produce.

Hitherto this truth, though more or less apparent to economic writers and thoughtful persons generally, has been apparent to them only by fits and starts, and has never been assigned any definite or logical place in their theories of production, or has ever been expressed clearly; and, owing to this cause, not only has it been entirely absent from the theories of the public generally, but its place has been usurped by a meaningless and absurd falsehood. In place of the living force Ability, residing in living men, popular thought, misled by a singular oversight of the economists, has substituted Capital—a thing which, apart from Ability, assists production as little as a dead or unborn donkey; and hence has arisen that dangerous and ridiculous illusion—sometimes plainly expressed, often only half-conscious—to the effect that if the labourers could only seize upon Capital they would be masters of the entire productive power of the country. The defenders of the existing system have been as guilty of this error as its antagonists; and the attack and defence have been conducted on equally false grounds. Thus in a recent strike, the final threat of the employers

Labour must remember that Ability is a living force which cannot be appropriated as Capital might be; but that it must be encouraged and propitiated.

—men who had created almost the whole of their enormous business — was that, if the strikers insisted upon certain demands, the Capital involved in the business would be removed to another country; and a well-known journal, professing to be devoted to the interest of Labour, conceived that it had disposed of this threat triumphantly by saying that, of the Capital a large part was not portable, and that the employers might go if they chose, and leave this behind. A great musician, who conceived himself to have been ill-treated in London, might just as well have threatened that he would remove his concert-room to St. Petersburg, when the principal meaning of his threat would be that he would remove *himself;* and the journal referred to might just as well have said, had the business in question been the production of a great picture, "The painter may go if he likes—what matter? We can keep his brushes."

The real parties, then, to the industrial disputes of the modern world are not active labourers on one side, and idle, perhaps idiotic owners of so much dead material on the other side: but they are, on the one side, the vast majority of men, possessed of average powers of production, and able to produce by them a comparatively small amount; and, on the other, a minority whose powers of production are exceptional, who, if we take the product of the average labourer as a unit, are able to multiply this to an almost indefinite extent, and who thus create an increasing store of Capital to be used by themselves, or transmitted to their representatives, and an increasing income to be divided between these and the labourers. In other words, the dispute is between the many who desire to increase their incomes, and the few by whose exceptional powers it is alone possible to increase them. Such has been the situation hitherto; it is such at the present moment; and the whole tendency of industrial progress is not to change, but to accentuate it. As the productivity of Human Exertion increases, the part played by Ability becomes more and more important. More and more do the average men become dependent on the exceptional men. So long as the nation at large remembers this, no reforms need be dreaded. If the nation forgets this, it will be in danger.

BOOK IV. CH. V.

In this view there is nothing derogatory to Labour.

every day of increasing, by its reforms, the very evils it wishes to obviate, and postponing or making impossible the advantages it wishes to secure.

And now let me pause to point out to the reader that to insist thus on the subordinate position of Labour as a productive agent is to insist on nothing that need wound the self-love of the labourers. In asserting that a man who can produce wealth only by Labour is inferior to a man who can produce ten times the amount by Ability, we assert his inferiority in the business of production only. In other respects he may be the better, even the greater man of the two. Shakespeare or Turner or Beethoven, if employed as producers of commodities, would probably have been no better than the ordinary hands in a factory, and far inferior to many a vulgar manufacturer. Again,—and it is still more important to notice this,—if we confine our attention to single commodities, many commodities produced by Labour[1]

[1] The reader must always bear in mind the definition given of Labour, as that kind of industrial exertion which is applied to one task at a time only, and while so applied begins and ends with that task; as distinguished from Ability, which influences simultaneously an indefinite number of tasks.

alone are better and more beautiful than any similar ones produced by Labour under the direction of Ability. Of some the reverse is true—notably those whose utility depends on their mechanical precision; but of others, in which beauty or even durability is of importance, such as fine stuffs or carpets, fine paper and printing, carved furniture, and many kinds of metal work, it is universally admitted that the handicraftsman, working under his own direction, was long ago able to produce results which Labour, directed by Ability, has never been able to improve upon, and is rarely able to equal. What Ability does is not to improve such commodities, but to multiply them, and thus convert them from rare luxuries into generally accessible comforts. A paraffin lamp, for instance, cast or stamped in metal, and manufactured by the thousand, might not be able to compare for beauty with a lamp of wrought iron, made by the skill and taste of some single unaided craftsman; but whereas the latter would probably cost several guineas, and be in reach only of the more opulent classes, the former would probably cost about half a crown, and, giving precisely as much

Ability does not improve the products of Labour, but multiplies them.

light as the other, would find its way into every cottage home, and take the place of a tallow dip or of darkness. Now since what the labouring classes demand in order to improve their position is not *better* commodities than can be produced by hand, but *more* commodities than can be produced by hand, Ability is a more important factor in the case than Labour; but none the less, from an artistic and moral point of view, the highest kind of Labour may stand higher than many of the most productive kinds of Ability.

Ability, in yielding up part of its proceeds to Labour, is discharging a moral debt.

Nor, again, do we ascribe to Labour any undignified position in insisting that much of its present income, and any possible increase of it, is and must be taken from the wealth produced by Ability. For even were there nothing more to be said than this, Labour is in a position, or we assume it will be, to command from Ability whatever sum may be in question, and can be neither despised nor blamed for making the best bargain for itself that is possible. But its position can be justified on far higher grounds than these. In the first place, Labour, by submitting itself to the guidance of Ability,—no matter whether the

OF ABILITY TO LABOUR

submission was voluntary, which it was not, or gradual, unconscious, and involuntary, which it was,—surrendered many conditions of life which were in themselves desirable, and has a moral claim on Ability to be compensated for having done so; whilst Ability, for its part, owes a moral debt to Labour, not upon this ground only, but on another also—one which thus far has never been recognised nor insisted on, but out of which arises a yet deeper and stronger obligation. I have shown that of the present annual wealth of the nation Ability creates very nearly two-thirds. But it may truly be said to have created far more than this. It may be said to have created not only two-thirds of the income, but also to have created two-thirds of the inhabitants. If the minority of this country, in pursuit of their own advantage, had not exercised their Ability and increased production as they have done, it is not too much to say that of our country's present inhabitants *twenty-four millions* would never have been in existence. Those, then, who either contributed to this result themselves, or inherit the Capital produced by those who did so, are burdened by the responsibility of having called these multitudes into life; and thus when the wages of Labour are augmented out of the proceeds of Ability, Ability is not robbed, nor does Labour accept a largess, but a duty is discharged which, if recognised for what it is, and performed in the spirit proper to it, will have the effect of really uniting classes, instead of that which is now so often aimed at—of confusing them.

<small>But Labour must not forget that it owes a debt to Ability;</small>
The labourers, on the other hand, must remember this: that having been called into existence, no matter by what means, and presumably wishing to live rather than be starved to death, they do not labour because the men of Ability make them, but—as I have before pointed out—because imperious Nature makes them; and that the tendency of Ability is in <small>And that this debt will grow heavier as the national wealth increases.</small> the long run to stand as a mediator between them and Nature, and whilst increasing the products of their Labour, to diminish its duration and severity.

There are two further points which yet remain to be noticed.

I have hitherto spoken of the increase of wealth and wages, as if that were the main object on which the labourers should concentrate their attention, and which bound up their interests so indissolubly with those of Ability. But it must also be pointed out that were Ability unduly hampered, and its efficacy enfeebled either by a diminution of its rewards, or by interference with its action, the question would soon arise, not of how to increase wages, but of how to prevent their falling. This point I have indeed alluded to already; but I wish now to exhibit it in a new light. As I mentioned in an earlier chapter, of the inhabitants of this country, who are something like *thirty-eight millions* in number, *twenty-six millions* live on imported corn, and about *thirteen millions* live on imported meat; or, to put it in another way, we all of us—the whole population—live on imported meat for nearly *five months* of the year, and on imported corn for *eight months*; and were these foreign food supplies interfered with, there are possibilities in this country of suffering, of famine, and of horror for all classes of society, to which the entire history of mankind offers us no parallel. This country, more than any country in the world, is an artificial fabric that has been built up by Ability, half of its present

BOOK IV.
CH. V.

wealth being,—let me repeat once more,—the marvellous product of the past fifty years; and the constant action of Ability is just as necessary to prevent this from dwindling as it is to achieve its increase. But in order that Ability may exert itself, something more is needed than mere freedom from industrial interference, or security for its natural rewards; and that is the maintenance of the national or international position which this country has secured for itself amongst the other countries of the world.

And this brings us round to what is commonly called Politics; which have, as this book will show, a far closer interest for the labourer than is commonly thought.

And this brings us to that class of questions which, in ordinary language, are called questions of policy, and amongst which foreign policy holds a chief place. Successful foreign policy means the maintenance or the achievement of those conditions that are most favourable to the industries of our own nation; and this means the conditions that are most favourable to the homes of our own people. It is too commonly supposed that the greatness and the ascendancy of our Empire minister to nothing but a certain natural pride; and natural pride, in its turn, is supposed by some to be an immoral and inhuman sentiment peculiar to the upper classes. No one will be quicker to resent this last ludicrous supposition than the great masses of the British people; but, all the same, they are apt to think the former supposition correct,—to regard the mere glory of the country as the principal result of our Empire; and such being the case, they are, on occasion, apt to be persuaded that glory can be bought at too dear a price, in money, struggle, or merely international friction. At all events, they are constantly tempted to regard foreign politics as something entirely disconnected with their own immediate, their domestic, their personal, their daily interests.

I am going to enter here on no debatable matter, nor discuss the value of this or that special possession, or this or that policy. It is enough to point out that, to a very great extent, on the political future of this country depends the magnitude of its income, and on the magnitude of its income depends the income of the working classes—the warmth of the hearth, the supply of food on the breakfast-table, of every labourer's home,—and that when popular support is asked for some foreign war, the sole immediate aim of which seems the defence of some remote frontier, or the maintenance of British prestige, it may well be that our soldiers will be really fighting for the safety and welfare of their children and wives at home—fighting to keep away from British and Irish doors not the foreign plunderer and the ravisher, but enemies still more pitiless—the want, the hunger, and the cold that spare neither age nor sex, and against which all prayers are unavailing.

THE END

PRINCIPLES OF
POLITICAL ECONOMY

By J. SHIELD NICHOLSON, M.A., D.Sc.

PROFESSOR OF POLITICAL ECONOMY IN THE UNIVERSITY OF EDINBURGH,
SOMETIME EXAMINER IN THE UNIVERSITIES OF CAMBRIDGE,
LONDON, AND VICTORIA

In 2 Vols. demy 8vo.
Vol. I. price 15s.

ALSO BY THE SAME AUTHOR

MONEY AND ESSAYS ON PRESENT MONETARY PROBLEMS

Second Edition, Revised and Enlarged.
In crown 8vo, price 7s. 6d.

HISTORY OF POLITICAL ECONOMY
ANCIENT, MEDIÆVAL, AND MODERN SCHOOLS

By J. KELLS INGRAM, LL.D.
FELLOW OF TRINITY COLLEGE, DUBLIN

In post 8vo, price 6s.

LONDON: A. & C. BLACK, SOHO SQUARE.

MANUALS OF PRACTICAL LAW

In crown 8vo, price 5s. each.

"It is better for a layman to go to a law-book than to go to law."—*Scotsman.*

The Volumes now published in this Series are:—

Banking and Negotiable Instruments.
By Frank Tillyard.

Bankruptcy.
By Charles F. Morrell.

Copyright and Patents.
By Wyndham Anstis Bewes, LL.B.

Education.
By James Williams, B.C.L., M.A.

Insurance.
By Charles F. Morrell.

Partnership and Companies.
By Percy F. Wheeler.

Wills and Intestate Succession.
By James Williams, B.C.L., M.A.

PRESS NOTICES.

"Well arranged."—*St. James's Gazette.*

"The series as a whole must prove of immense service to the classes mentioned, as well as to accountants, trustees, factors, agents, and others."—*Glasgow Herald.*

"Deservedly popular."—*Eastern Morning News.*

"Excellent."—*Observer.*

"Admirable five-shilling series."—*Freeman's Journal.*

"A well-arranged series at a uniform price, and possessing certain distinct advantages in regard to method of treatment and style."—*Liverpool Mercury.*

"We wish Messrs. Black's admirable little series well."—*Law Notes.*

"A series whose issues so far are undoubtedly of great value to the financial, commercial, and trading communities."—*Liverpool Post.*

"The manuals, if used as they are intended to be, ought certainly to be found of great assistance."—*Whitehall Review.*

London: A. & C. BLACK, Soho Square.

A
HISTORY OF SOCIALISM

BY

THOMAS KIRKUP

In crown 8vo, 300 pages, price 6s.

"So fair, so learned, and so well written, that we have nothing but praise for its author."—*Athenæum*.

"No better book for the purpose has come under our notice than Mr. Kirkup's new work, 'A History of Socialism.'"—*The World*.

"This bold and luminous outline displays an uncommon grasp of the underlying principles of a movement which is rapidly beginning to play a great part in modern society."—*Standard*.

"A very valuable and useful epitome."—*Glasgow Herald*.

"It is a work of true value and present importance."—*Evening News and Post*.

"Well written, clear, tolerant, intelligible to all cultivated people."—*Daily Chronicle*.

"Should be on the shelves of every public library and every working-men's club."—*Pall Mall Gazette*.

"The tone of this able and opportune volume is at once sympathetic, independent, and fearless."—*Leeds Mercury*.

"Well worthy to remain the standard text-book on Socialism."—*British Weekly*.

"Marked by great candour and much independence of thought, as well as by a wide knowledge of his subject."—*Newcastle Leader*.

"Practically indispensable to any one who wishes to acquire an adequate grasp of the leading phases of historic socialism."—*Freeman's Journal*.

"Sound, original work."—*Aberdeen Free Press*.

"Nothing could be more timely than Mr. Kirkup's very able and lucid though concise 'History of Socialism.'"—*Literary World*.

"Apropos of Socialism, I do not know where you will find a more brilliant account or a more lucid criticism of this on-coming movement than in Mr. Thomas Kirkup's 'History of Socialism.'"—*Truth*.

LONDON : A. & C. BLACK, SOHO SQUARE.

THE PROCESS OF ARGUMENT

A CONTRIBUTION TO LOGIC

In crown 8vo, price 5s.

MARRIAGE & FAMILY RELATIONS

By NEVILL GEARY.

In large crown 8vo, price 12s. 6d.

HISTORICAL INTRODUCTION TO THE PRIVATE LAW OF ROME

By Prof. JAMES MUIRHEAD, LL.D.

In demy 8vo, price 21s.

LONDON: A. & C. BLACK, SOHO SQUARE.

www.ingramcontent.com/pod-product-compliance
Lightning Source LLC
Chambersburg PA
CBHW030308240426
43673CB00040B/1095